The Needs of Teachers

Edited by

V. Alan McClelland and Ved Varma

CASSELL

Cassell
Wellington House
125 Strand
London WC2R 0BB

127 West 24th Street
New York
NY 10011

British Library Cataloguing-in-Publication Data
A catalogue record for this book is available from the British Library.

Library of Congress Cataloging-in-Publication Data
The needs of teachers / edited by V. Alan McClelland and Ved Varma.
      p. cm. — (Cassell education)
   Includes bibliographical references and index.
   ISBN 0-304-33334-4. — ISBN 0-304-33335-2
   1. Teachers — Great Britain. 2. Teachers — In-service training—
Great Britain. 3. Teacher morale — Great Britain. 4. Teaching —
– Vocational guidance — Great Britain. I. McClelland. V. A. (Vincent
Alan) II. Varma, Ved P.   III. Series.
LB1775.4.G7N44   1996
371.1' 00941—dc20   96-26740
                                                              CIP

ISBN   0-304-333344 (hardback)
          0-304-333352 (paperback)

Typeset by Action Typesetting Ltd, Gloucester
Printed and bound in Great Britain by Redwood Books, Trowbridge, Wiltshire

Contents

For Alkelda

Notes on Contributors

Horace Bennett is a Principal Lecturer in Education Management in the School of Professional Education and Development at Leeds Metropolitan University. He has previously published a book on appraisal. His main research is in the appraisal field, although he has lectured on change management over a five-year period on Masters degree courses. He spent twenty years in schools as a head of English and a Sixth Form director.

Ron Best is Assistant Dean and Professor of Education at Roehampton Institute, London. He has researched and published on numerous aspects of education, including teachers' caring roles and the organization of provision for children with learning difficulties in mainstream classrooms. He is a founder member of the National Association for Pastoral Care in Education (NAPCE) and Executive Editor of its journal. He is co-editor of Cassell *Studies in Pastoral Care and Personal and Social Education*, and of two recent books in the field: *Caring for Children* (with P. Lang and A. Lichtenberg, 1994) and *Pastoral Care and Personal-Social Education: Entitlement and Provision* (with P. Lang, C. Lodge and C. Watkins, 1995), both published by Cassell.

V. Alan McClelland is Professor of Educational Studies and Dean of the School of Education at Hull University. He has held appointments in three universities, two of them chairs, and has worked in a variety of schools and a College of Education. He has published widely in the history and philosophy of education, religious education and ecclesiastical history. His publications include two major books by Oxford University Press and many contributions to books and collections of essays. He currently edits two international journals and is preparing for publication a major historical study of the years 1935–75.

Mick McManus has taught in schools for twenty years and is now in charge of secondary education at Leeds Metropolitan University. He is author of *Troublesome Behaviour in the Classroom: Meeting Individual Needs* (Routledge, 1995) and a series of textbooks for lower-attaining secondary pupils: the *Foundation for Life* series (Hodder, 1991).

Carl Parsons has written on curriculum change, evaluation and quality assurance. His current research interests are in the field of welfare policy with a particular focus on inter-agency work to address problems presented by excluded children and pupil disaffection.

John Sayer directs the EU TEMPUS Project: *Developing Schools for Democracy in Europe*, from the University of Oxford. Previously Head of Minehead School and Principal of Banbury School, he was President of the Secondary Heads Association, before running the Education Management Unit in the University of London. He edits the Cassell *Education Management* series, was Founder-Secretary and is now Vice-Chair of the General Teaching Council initiative for England and Wales.

Brian Spence is a Senior Lecturer in the School of Education at the University of Hull and Organizer for In-Service Education. His specialism is educational management and administration with particular research interests in staff roles, consultation and decision-making in schools. He is particularly committed to working with teachers off-site on professional development activities both in the UK and abroad.

Ved Varma was an educational psychologist with Richmond and Brent. Now retired, he formerly worked at the Tavistock Clinic in London and he has published extensively on educational topics over many years.

Anne Waterhouse has been headteacher at Asmall County Primary School in Lancashire since January 1984. She is a member of the Executive of the National Union of Teachers and is Vice-Chair of the Union's Education and Equal Opportunities Committee but writes here in a personal capacity. Over the years she has been involved with initial teacher education at Edge Hill College of Higher Education and with the delivery of in-service activities for teachers and non-teaching staff for Lancashire, the Isle of Man and Gwent LEAs as well as through the NUT National Education Conference.

Preface

V. Alan McClelland

The contributors to this volume are concerned with what are the constituents of a good education and with the qualities of a good teacher. William Walsh, employing a Coleridgean analysis, described a good education as persisting 'not as a collection of information' but 'as a certain unity of self, more or less coherent, more or less rich, and as a certain method of thinking and feeling, more or less complex, more or less sensitive' (William Walsh in *Higher Education*, ed. J. Lawlor, 1972). He continued that 'what lasts, what enters into us as a result of school and college, is a certain kind of charged awareness, a blend of value, attitude and assumption, a certain moral tone, a special quality of imagination, a particular flavour of sensibility.' From this, John Passmore's definition of the good teacher follows: 'whether a teacher has a "certificate" to mark the fact that he has acquired certain skills is much less important than that he knows what he is talking about and cares about his pupils learning what he hopes to teach them' (John Passmore in *The Philosophy of Teaching*, 1980).

The first essay in this volume relates to both these complementary definitions and argues that government and teacher-training agencies have lost their way in following a faulty conceptualization of teacher education and training, a point emphasized by the weakening of the links with higher education on the one hand and by the vacillating view of the fundamental unity and cohesion of education on the other. The two-pronged loss of direction has led to a process of deprofessionalization of teachers with which John Sayer is concerned. There ought to be no dichotomy between considering teaching as a vocation and approaching it as a craft.

One of the conditions affecting the loss of a consciousness of professionality is not unrelated to changes in pay bargaining and conditions of service. Recent plans for differential modes of training for teachers of children in the early years of schooling, in particular, have brought uncertainty and unease into the profession. A Lancashire head-teacher in primary education, Anne Waterhouse, is well placed to consider this issue from the teacher's viewpoint. Both Horace Bennett and Carl Parsons are concerned in their respective chapters with the management of change in the teaching profession and with the development of tactics to cope with the altering environment of teaching and learning in contemporary schools. It is in this matter that the in-service education of teachers has a major role to play. Dr Brian Spence locates the objectives of INSET firmly within the context of developing the 'reflective practitioner', an aim in which in-service education can relate to processes of initial teacher preparation and induction. INSET has a function to play in clearly defining the sub-roles teachers have to assume and Ron Best attempts to consider these as 'the socially constructed products of interaction between individuals with professional responsibilities and general aspirations.' Mick McManus, in his concluding chapter, is concerned with the maintenance of morale among teachers and especially with the contribution of policy-makers and politicians, in both positive and negative ways, in influencing the morale of teachers.

Chapter 1

Quality and Initial Teacher Education

V. Alan McClelland

Peter Scott has charged Thatcherism with 'the attempted destruction' of a delicate values system that long underpinned Britain's success in higher education (Scott, 1988, p.142). Although not specifically referring to teacher education, his stricture gained a specific coherence when applied to Thatcherite policies towards the formation and preparation of teachers. Quality of training and versatility of emphasis have been tightly yoked to the rods of bureaucratic regulation, central direction and control. The characteristically British concepts of checks and balances, based upon subscription to an already operative philosophy of partnership with schools, have been eroded with a ruthlessness in intensity and scale. The weakening of an ideal of partnership in education between central and local government agencies, between an independent, informal inspectorate and the schools, between teachers, their professional associations and national bargaining bodies over pay and conditions of service has been a marked feature of the years since the beginning of the second Thatcher administration of 1983.

The substitution of confrontational for consensual approaches in education, however, has inconsistently been accompanied by a demand for a greater degree of association between the providers of initial teacher education and the schools in which pre-service teachers gain their needed practical initiation into teaching, a demand which has paid scant regard to the high degree of co-operation already in operation. But even Thatcher's own original concept of partnership in teacher education has now been put at risk by a measure of self-destruction in the pursuit of her creed of 1984, encapsulated in the statement that 'the effective monopoly exercised by the existing teacher-training routes had to be broken' (Thatcher, 1993, p. 598) in pursuit of the desirable goal of gladiatorial ethics and the competition of the market-place. Consequently the idea of a closer partnership between schools and providers of initial teacher education, which seemed a logical truism to many, was dealt a further blow by the establishment of a new Teacher Training Agency (TTA) charged, as part of its *raison d'être*, with encouraging the growth of initiatives in which schools themselves would become, increasingly, sole providers of teacher training, eschewing any obeisance at the altar of partnership. This parvenu philosophy of teacher education, therefore, based upon the twin shibboleths of the market-place and competitive efficiency, masquerading under the slogan of quality, has taken on an unproven theological orthodoxy. One is reminded of the warning of the late Douglas Woodruff in quoting Macaulay in the last century and Inge in this century 'that our society would be destroyed not by external invaders as in the Dark Ages, but by the barbarians in our midst, those whom we would ourselves nurture' (Craig, 1978, p.178). To this statement Woodruff prophetically remarked: 'this is plainly what is happening with education.'

The report of the National Commission on Education (NCE), an independent inquiry into the long-term development of education and training in the United Kingdom, listed half-a-dozen desiderata for teaching performance in schools to improve. Ahead of new proposed arrangements for better pay, career progression and working conditions are listed two constitutive elements that have long been accepted as crucial by teacher educators if professionalism was to be seen to advance among teachers. These were 'a spiral of raised standards of entrants to teaching and the promotion of a high status profession' with 'an entitlement for every teacher to rigorous training and development throughout his or her career.' Associated with these factors were 'a strengthening of the primary role of the teacher as an educator, in command of a range of expertise and with appropriate technological back-ups', 'coherent leadership throughout the profession, including self-regulation' and 'equality of opportunity for all staff' (NCE, 1993, p.233). Initial teacher education (ITT) was seen as the foundation stone upon which all other developments must rest, although it was clearly stated 'this cannot be judged in terms of the degree to which it turns out teachers prepared for the whole of their working lives, since that would ignore what can be achieved through subsequent training and development' (NCE, 1993, p.212). Nevertheless, it concluded 'a rigorous period of training and education is essential for anyone entering a profession not least teaching, and this is reflected in the fact that most industrialised countries are increasing the amount of training that teachers receive'. Significantly, the report considered that 'there seems to be no doubt that the most successful teacher training occurs when there is a genuine partnership between school and higher education institution, each playing a distinctive part according to strength, reinforcing the work of the other' (NCE, 1993, p.214). Mindful of the fact that university involvement in teacher education was already present, in varying degrees, in most countries of Europe, the continued involvement of higher education institutions in the United Kingdom in teacher education was seen as necessary to provide 'the theoretical base' from which 'students can plan work and approach classes with more confidence', having gained 'some knowledge of how children learn and which methods have been found successful in different circumstances.'

Mechanistic and utilitarian as this concept of the contribution of higher education to teacher training may be, by means of which 'theory and practice' might hopefully 'reinforce each other', it is not dissimilar from the concepts finding their application in a variety of European countries, including, for example, Austria, France and Spain. There is a difference of emphasis, in attitude, however, between the approach adopted in the United Kingdom and that of these European countries, a point recently highlighted by Anthony Greaves. He perceives the philosophy of British universities as being driven by a 'reforming' impulse, an encouragement of young people 'to question everything before accepting or rejecting it', a philosophy which is indicative of why the British government, with its current subscription to centralist ideology, is antipathetic to university involvement in teacher education. The tradition of the Continent, more conservative and humanistic in outlook, does not present the same degree of threat to politicians bent upon social engineering. Questioning and debate by young teachers is seen in England 'as a threat to the *status quo*', whereas the introduction of a fully school-based mechanistic process of teacher education, charged only with the delivery of the national curriculum and its objectives in schools, already 'sanitized' by government directives, is not likely to challenge current orthodoxies. 'Sitting by Nelly' and imitating what Nelly does cannot conceivably constitute a threat to anybody (Greaves, 1994, p.104).

The deprofessionalization of teachers by means of impoverished approaches to pre-service training and subsequent induction procedures has been a marked feature of Conservative Party policy, based upon a fear of open discussion in the educative process. By making it difficult, if not impossible, for providing institutions, in the limited time at their disposal, to do more than supply programmes in methods of teaching and classroom management skills, the government's ideological bandwagon, supported by rigid systems of OFSTED inspections and frequent so-called 'quality' evaluations, has succeeded in leaving little opportunity for aspirants to the teaching profession to think, to debate or to question fundamental issues about the meaning and purpose of what they are to engage themselves upon in a lifetime of service to children. Furthermore, students have little time or opportunity to come to grips with the psychological and sociological mores necessary for an effective training process to proceed. The mere mention of the 'ologies', or of sufficient time being given to the study of the philosophical, historical, psychological or sociological understanding of teaching and its processes within a teacher-formation programme, is likely to drive the average Conservative politician into a paroxysm of rage and denunciation and yet the point John Passmore made over a decade ago is as valid today as it was then: 'if a man were to call himself an economist and then it were to be discovered that he had never heard of marginal utility, was wholly ignorant of the work of Keynes, had no knowledge of economic theory and had acquired no skill as a economic analyst, he would at once be denounced as an impostor' (Passmore, 1980, p.3). Part of the malaise among teachers today, in their struggle to come to grips with a plethora of social, learning and behavioural problems in the classroom is brought about because they lack the adequate theoretical framework within which their particular problems can be located and because they are ill-prepared to view the concept of teaching in relation to its extensive human, moral, social and scientific hinterland. As Passmore argued 'the view that what is taught, always, is how to do something is as untenable as the view that what is taught, always, is a formally structured subject.' To produce a teaching profession less knowledgeable about the nature of its own professionalism and less able to speak with authority on the constituents of the teaching and learning process, one less exposed to recent research processes and research findings, one discouraged by overload in working conditions from reading widely and yet selectively about professional concerns, is to render a serious disservice to both children and parents. Indeed it makes a mockery of the advocacy of parental choice because such teachers are unlikely to effect that improvement in the quality of teaching that parents are reputedly seeking. It also will fail to achieve the government's evident quest to establish a secure base for an élitism in talent and influence. Chesterton put the heart of the problem very well when he asserted that man has no alternative but to be influenced by thought that has been thought out or by thought that has not been thought out. The point is reinforced by that contemporary guru of the political right, Anthony O'Hear, writing some 14 years ago, when he declared 'the lack of final authorities in any area, and the advocacy of pluralism in theories, beliefs and life-styles, mean that although we are attempting to teach children existing methods and theories, we should want at least some of those we teach eventually to criticise what already exists and to improve on it. But, as with choice, satisfactory and constructive criticism can be made only on the basis of an understanding of what is being chosen or criticised' (O'Hear, 1981, p.89). O'Hear's point cannot be achieved without appropriate steps being taken to secure a thoughtful and intellectually well-equipped teaching force. Harry Schofield produced an excellent image which vividly encapsulated this point:

> when the motor mechanic puts a new part into an engine, he attaches one unthinking object to another. He can do it only one particular way, and does it in the same way every time. If he did not, the part would not fit into the engine. But the teacher is an individual and each child is an individual. For each the same subject matter may have different meanings, or no meaning at all, or profound meaning. It is absurd to suggest that providing teachers with 'knack' or 'skill' can be called 'teacher education'.
>
> (Schofield, 1972, p.52)

He shows how ridiculous it is to claim 'we must *educate* our electorate, *educate* our rulers and *educate* good citizens and then claim that we should concentrate on *training* teachers, as distinct from *educating* them.'

It is noticeable that some of main defenders of the role of universities and higher education institutions in teacher education, when dealing with the concept of partnership with schools, have also neglected to grasp the fundamental significance of this training/educating dichotomy. Lord Judd, in his opening speech in the House of Lords on 14 March 1994, on the second day of the committee stage of the education bill then before Parliament, began in impeccable fashion. Successfully moving an amendment designed to ensure that teacher formation, as distinct from training in its narrower connotation, should remain at the heart of any working partnership between schools and higher education, he said:

> Teaching is not just a mechanical process by which the curriculum is delivered to pupils. It is absolutely essential that the teacher is reflective and creative; that he or she is master of the subject being taught and preferably with a passion for it. That will become even more essential with the pressures of the century ahead. To encourage thoughtful and creative pupils, demands the same qualities of those who teach them; and in order to develop those qualities teachers need some theoretical framework within which to consider children's development, addressing their needs and making appropriate judgements about the curriculum.
>
> (*Hansard*, House of Lords, 14 March 1994, Clause 11)

Important as that affirmation was there was little else in the debate that showed an understanding of the nature of the complex process of teacher education other than the expression of a widely held view that 'it is the higher education institutions which can provide quality control for courses and for the qualifications awarded at the end of these courses.' In the whole of the debate, indeed, there was nothing about the need for coherence in teacher education, about the essential *unity* of the educative process, about aims and ends. There was no evidence of what Robin Barrow once described as 'clear ideas about what schooling is for', about 'clear and rational argument, and clear conceptions of education, morality, intelligence and other ideas that are central to the enterprise' (Barrow, 1981, p.202). No construction of 'partnership' schemes *per se* between schools and higher education establishments can deliver such objectives; they relate to the content and methodology of teacher education, not to the world of administrative organization and skills provision. To Earl Russell, speaking in the same parliamentary debate as Judd, co-operation with an institute of higher education was needed to confer 'companionship, advice, counselling and a degree of safety net', an impoverishment of argument that betrayed sympathy for the providers but showed little genuine understanding of the heart of the teacher education operation.

Weak as some of the arguments used in the parliamentary debate on the 1994 education bill seemed to be, they were supportive of the opposition to the bill of bodies and organizations concerned more immediately with the processes of the formation of teachers. Some of the latter were convinced of the concept of 'open professionalism', as enunciated by the OECD, an idea in which is enshrined the belief that 'the modern teacher, at the focal point of rapidly changing and highly demanding educational policies needs to be both open to communal influence and co-operation – with colleagues, the school, on-going research and developments, parents, the community – and to receive respect as an individual professional' (OECD, 1990). Sir William Taylor would accept that viewpoint. As former chairman of the now defunct Council for the Accreditation of Teacher Education (CATE) he has declared that 'the expectation that trainee teachers should be taught to be analytical and critical is not a conspiracy to turn them into political radicals. It is teaching them a proper part of their rôle as a teacher', for 'they must be able to analyse what they are doing' (*Report*, 1994, p.2). Essentially the same point was at the heart of a statement issued by the Early Childhood Education organization when it commented that 'proposals to transfer the central responsibility for development and running courses to schools are shortsighted and unrealistic' because 'partnerships between schools and institutions of higher education is the key to developing teachers' understanding of the links between theory and practice' (Early Childhood Education's *Statement on the 1994 Education Bill*, National Children's Bureau, 1994). The joint statement of the AUT, NATFHE, SCOP and UCET (*1994 Education Bill. Response* etc, 1994) commented on 'the narrow view of "training"' embodied in the government's proposals to permit the development of fully school-based courses which 'would narrow the scope and reduce the quality of teacher education' at a time when 'the breadth of view and critical scrutiny of evidence which Higher Education provides are essential components in their initial training and continuing professional development.' The various teachers' organizations indicating that 'demands made on schools are constantly rising and higher levels of professional knowledge and competence are required of all teachers' emphasized that the teaching profession 'depends upon an expanding and lively higher education sector for research and independent inquiry, for the dissemination of best practice and for links with other related disciplines, to prevent its isolation and to provide the challenge of new ideas' (The Teachers' Organizations: *Statement on the 1994 Education Bill*, 1994). The National Association of Governors and Managers doubted whether schools could enable student teachers 'to become reflective and self-critical professionals with a proper understanding of how children learn' under the new proposed arrangements of either the 'partnership' or 'whole school' varieties (*Education Bill, 1994. Comments by the National Association of Governors and Managers*, 1994). Parents' organizations, for their part, saw the possible non-involvement of higher education institutions in teacher education as undermining 'the status of teaching' (*Statement on the 1994 Education Bill from ACE, CASE, NAPE and NCPTA*, 1994). The Teacher Education Alliance was even more explicit, teaching being considered as being 'too complex' and good teaching 'too dependent on professional self-awareness' for preparation 'to be reduced to a narrow form of training, based on the mere acquisition of techniques.' Teaching 'must be fully informed by the research and independent inquiry which helps to identify and disseminate good practice' (*Government Proposals for Initial Teacher Training*. Response of NCPTA, CASE, NAGM, NUT, NASUWT, ATL, PAT, COSTA, SHA, NAHT, General Teaching Council of England and Wales, HMC, GSA, CVCP, UCET, AUT, NATFHE, BERA, AMA, ACC, FCFC, TUC, NUS, CEA and NAPPCE, 1994).

Underlying the worries articulated by such a wide variety of interests and organizations in British life, an opposition ignored by government as of little significance, was the rarely articulated concern that the government's vision of the future of teacher education and its organizational structure gave scant regard to the essential unity of education itself. By 'unity of education' is meant that education is a self-consistent activity, a cohesive function that implies not only the integration of theory and practice but also an integration which is purposeful and directed at specific and clearly recognized aims and objectives. Education forms a unity with the life of an individual exposed to its influence. The point is well illustrated in an analogy devised by Glenn Langford:

> the functioning of an organ is judged by its contribution to the survival of the system constituted by the whole body of which it is a part. Organs of perception make their contribution by informing the organism of the situation in which it is placed. Eyes which perform well, therefore, tell you what is there. And what is there can be decided not by an examination of the physical process which occurs in perception but by reference to the public world which exists independently of those processes.
>
> (Langford, 1975, p.80)

The lack, then, of a concept of unity for education and educational processes is associated with a failure to ask the right question which underpins all that to which education is designed to relate. Antonio Rosmini-Serbati in the nineteenth century put the point with maximum clarity when he declared 'by education ... I mean that which leads a man to the highest point of moral perfection possible to him ... by means of a well-ordered development and harmonious cultivation of all his faculties' (Rosmini-Serbati, 1887–94, X, p.739).

When Peter Scott wrote of the Thatcherite attempt to destroy a delicate values system driving Britain's earlier success in higher education, he did not significantly identify the cult of individualism as the main agent of corruption. This cult lies at the heart of Conservative governmental reform in teacher education and its effect has been witnessed in all levels of educational provision. The benchmarks are competitiveness, personal ambition and the loss of a non-personal idealism. The cult of individualism, like the American-style hedonistic cult of the human body, must not be confused with a proper subscription to the importance of personality. A truly attractive personality is one which is *governed by* a guiding principle which keeps in proper relationship personal attributes and skills. It is in the development of personality, not individualism, that we come to the heart of the unity of education, a bringing together of moral, physical and intellectual development in meaningful and conscious relationship. A theory of education based upon such a philosophy must, of necessity, value the development of human beings in their wholeness. Mary Warnock issued a timely caution against the pursuit by the state of paternalistic concepts of individualism when she wrote that society at large should not forget that it was for people in society that education existed, 'in order to fulfil *their* wants and aspirations' (Warnock, 1977, p. 170). She argued 'the teacher is responsible not only for the child's learning what is contained in the curriculum but also, in part, for his learning to behave well, to become morally good.' This is something which cannot be taught as part of set timetabled periods and it is something which teacher-training institutions in the past have, by and large, ignored or dealt with badly. The reason for this cannot be ascribed to a single source but it has certainly been affected by the Thatcherite philosophy in its attack on the concept of society as an organic and living reality. Margaret Thatcher articulated the teaching as 'there are individual men and women, and there are families. And no government can do anything except through people, and people must look to themselves first. It's our duty to look after ourselves and then to look after our neighbours' (Thatcher, 1993, p. 626). This raw and rugged appeal to individualism and human self-ishness conflicts profoundly with Warnock s view that 'it is less important to form judgements about education itself than about the life to which it is all leading' (Warnock, 1977, p. 173). Teachers have 'to think about what one hopes' for children 'when their education is over.' In essence, education can thus be defined as 'the application of a philosophy of life to the upbringing of children (O'Leary, n.d, p. 17). For the Christian or for the Muslim this philosophy of life will have a specific connotation, for others it will rest in their definition 'of man's ultimate worth and personal value.' Rosmini went to the heart of the matter:

> One of the most common defects I have noticed in the various educational systems is that none of them defines clearly the end to which all educational efforts ought to be directed. Education as a result becomes vacillatory, useless, and even harmful. If the end is not fully determined and defined, one is not in a position to choose the most appropriate means to that end. If education does not serve its legitimate purpose it is useless: if it leads children away from their proper end, it is harmful.
>
> (O'Leary, n.d., p. 17)

Rosmini wrote of 'a well-ordered development and harmonious cultivation of all (a man's) faculties' as the source of unity in the educative process and an aim which should find widespread subscription. He maintained that not only must the education of the individual have a perfect unity but 'all the efforts of the educator and all the means he uses must, with perfect coherence and consistency contribute to this end.' And the end is moral. Philip May, from the stance of a lifetime's involvement in the education of teachers, has developed the point that 'a rightly oriented education will present to children the fact that responsible choices must be made, choices not just about careers but about attitudes to others, about friends, about one's mode of living, and about the belief by which one intends to live' (May, 1972, pp. 52–3).

It is, of course, in the concern of analysing the unity and aim of education that institutions of higher education are themselves clearly deficient. If teacher–educators lack understanding and vision of the wider outreach of education, they cannot articulate a coherent view of the task confronting them. They take refuge, rather, within a mish-mash of curriculum presentations and methodological skills. Over many years of interviewing for lectureships in Education, the writer has grown accustomed to the look of blank incomprehension when an aspirant for a post is asked to talk a little about his/her philosophy of education or is requested to comment upon the importance of aims and purpose or values in the provision of teacher education. Part of the problem has been generated by the undue emphasis upon methodology in the training of teachers, as if the major role of teachers was concerned solely with the devising of communicative skills in biology or history or design technology. The iconoclastic destruction of courses in the philosophy of education and in the historical, sociological and psychological foundations of education has left a yawning abyss which has not been bridged. Consequently there is a passion among teacher–educators for preparing students only to deliver the National Curriculum and concentrate upon its various attainment targets. This is done well but it lacks any recognition of what Fred Inglis has warned when he wrote 'by implying a view of what to do with knowledge, the curriculum, like the culture, implies a picture of how to live and who to be; even in liberal society, it adumbrates the passages of the good life, in private and in public (and how the two are divided), and it proposes a structure of the self in relation to this praxis' (Inglis, 1985, p. 49). The teachers of the future need a new vision from teacher–educators that enables them to raise themselves above their environment and realize they can become agents of change in the world, while still preparing themselves to take a specific place in it.

The concept of partnership, if it is to restore a proper perspective to the formation and training of teachers, necessitates a radical look. University schools of education and those of other institutions should retain a nucleus of permanent staff whose function it would be to add unity and purpose to the role of teacher education. To this end each of these lecturers should be required to spend a year in every five years of contractual service working in schools, a period of secondment in which they could gain valuable additional experience and reinvestigate their teaching, writing and research. This nucleus of staff would not be concerned with the teaching of method, as such, the latter being provided by good school teachers seconded from schools and selected for their vision of what it means to be a good teacher–educator and who would spend no longer than three years in the training institute before returning to the classroom. This structured cross-fertilization, spelling the end of the old-style method tutor, would be beneficial to schools and to teacher education, leading to a reflowering of research and classroom investigation. It would be a much closer partnership than is currently in evidence and one based upon a perceived unity of purpose. It would bring an element of practical classroom experience into the in-service education programmes of universities and higher education institutions and, by the process of regular return to the classroom, its experiences would constitute a valuable in-service education programme in itself. In such a way there would be a rapid advance to Patricia Broadfoot's ideal of the teacher 'who has a framework of reference which enables him to understand the *rationale* of his/her work and its challenges, is able to draw on research findings in the professional decisions relating to practice and is able and willing to contribute to on-going policy and emerging initiative' (Broadfoot, 1992).

The form of partnership outlined above would lead to a greater sharing of common goals and objectives for teacher education and an intensive drive on the part of teachers and teacher–educators to reflect anew upon their own cherished practices and the need for them. This development of partnership would obviate the worst excesses of the discredited apprenticeship models and put the soul back into teacher education in which partnership would be visibly seen to bring together complementary strengths within a context of realization of the importance of educational aims and unity of conception. Tony Edwards recently emphasized the point that 'training too narrowly centred on the here-and-how is open to the charge of parochialism, leaving students under-prepared to cope with very different circumstances and under-informed about wider influences on their work' (Edwards, 1990, p. 187). Now is the time to do something about it!

REFERENCES

Barrow, R. (1981) *The Philosophy of Schooling*. Brighton: Wheatsheaf.

Broadfoot, P. (1992) 'Educational research in relation to teacher education.' Lyons: ATEE, Seminar Paper.

Craig, M. (1978) *Woodruff at Random*. London: The Universe.

Education Bill (1994) Statements from Early Childhood Education Organizations; Higher Education (Association of University Teachers; National Association of Teachers in Further and Higher Education; Standing Conference of Principals of Higher Education Colleges and the Universities' Council for the Education of Teachers); The Teachers' Organizations (Association of Teachers and Lecturers; National Association of Headteachers; National Association of Schoolmasters/Union of Women Teachers; National Union of Teachers; Professional Association of Teachers; Secondary Heads Association); School Governors and Managers (National Association); Advisory Centre for Education, Campaign for State Education, National Association for Primary Education, National Confederation of Parent/Teacher Associations; Teacher Education Alliance (National Confederation of Parent/Teacher Associations; Campaign for State Education; National Association of Governors and Managers); the various teacher associations – NUT, NASUWT, ATL, PAT, COSTA, SHA, NAHT and the General Teaching Council, England and Wales; Headmasters' Conference; Girls' Schools Association; Universities and Higher Education Institutions – CVCP, UCET, AUT, NATFHE; The British Educational Research Association; Local Authorities – AMA, ACC; Free Church Federal Council; TUC; NUS; Council for Educational Advance; National Association for Pastoral Care in Education.

Edwards, T. (1990) 'Schools of education – their work and their future.' In J. B. Thomas (ed.) *British Universities and Teacher Education: A Century of Change*. London: The Falmer Press.

Greaves, A. E. (1994) 'Teacher education in France: an intruder's view.' In T. Sander (ed.) *Current Changes and Challenges in European Teacher Education*. Bruxelles: RIF, Réseau d'Institutions De Formation – Sub Network 4.

Hansard (1994) House of Lords, Education Bill, 14 March.

Inglis, F. (1985) *The Management of Ignorance*. Oxford: Basil Blackwell.

Langford, G. (1975) 'Education and human being II'. In S. C. Brown, (ed.) *Philosophers Discuss Education*. London: Macmillan.

May, P. (1972) *Which Way to School?* Berkhamsted: Lion.

NCE (National Commission on Education) (1993) *Learning to Succeed*. Report of the Paul Hamlyn Foundation. London: Heinemann.

OECD (1990) *The Teacher Today*. Paris: OECD.

O'Hear, A. (1981) *Education, Society and Human Nature*. London: Routledge and Kegan Paul.

O'Leary, K. (n.d.) *Rosmini's Educational Thought*. Omeath: privately published.

Passmore, J. (1980) *The Philosophy of Teaching*. London: Duckworth.

Report (1994) *Journal of the Association of Teachers and Lecturers*, **1**   **6** (3). Interview with Sir William Taylor.

Rosmini-Serbati, A. (1887–94) *Epistolario completo di Antonio Rosmini-Serbati* (13 vols). Casale: Giovanni Pane.

Schofield, H. (1972) *The Philosophy of Education*. London: George Allen and Unwin.

Scott, P. (1988) 'Higher education'. In M. Morris and C. Griggs, (eds) *Education – The Wasted Years? 1973–1986*. London: The Falmer Press.

Thatcher, M. (1993) *The Downing Street Years*. London: HarperCollins.

Warnock, M. (1977) *Schools of Thought*. London: Faber and Faber.

Chapter 2

The Need for Recognition and Professional Status

John Sayer

INTRODUCTION

The words of this chapter title are charged with deeply felt meanings, which have to be recognized even if not rigorously defined. The chapter will outline UK aspirations towards professional recognition. The Scottish example will be considered. Current moves towards a GTC in England and Wales will be considered, in the wake of government attempts to deprofessionalize.

Teaching is both a calling and a craft. Its activities are related to generally recognized definitions of a 'profession'. In this chapter, the gap is explored between present circumstances and those necessary for public recognition as a profession. The pursuit of a full educating profession will not be confined to those teaching in schools. The distinction is to be drawn between traditional professionalism and an open professionality more appropriate for present expectations.

Professional needs are closely related to morale. Teachers need the confidence and trust of those they serve and schools need to have the understanding, confidence and support of the public at large. Equally, the public needs to have confidence in schools and teachers in general, whilst parents and students need to have trust and confidence in individual teachers.

There has to be a shared sense of purpose across government political trends for teachers and schools to be confident that their mission makes sense in the society to which young people are to contribute. There must be a framework in which to share that sense of purpose.

Professional needs are related to responsibility. Teachers need to have professional scope and space, to educate according to trained insights into students' learning. They need to have ownership of the teaching task. They need to feel responsible and professionally accountable for the quality of service provided.

The need will be considered for parity of esteem with other callings, along with the peculiarly British professional class. Statutory bodies for other professions will be referred to, and some differences among them described. Professional recognition is to be distinguished from social and economic recognition. The British scene will be related to international concerns, in particular European Union concerns for the status of teachers, in the convening of different contexts and traditions, as we address the needs of a shared or common future.

WORDS AND THEIR ASSOCIATIONS

Without wishing to impose a particular meaning on the words which constitute the title of this chapter, I want at least to acknowledge that the four nouns, need, recognition, status and indeed teachers are each used with different mixtures of felt understandings. Even if this may be obvious, it is important to keep it constantly in mind if offering a general view.

Need

A need may be perceived and wanted by the subject, or identified by others. Special educational needs, for example, are usually of the latter variety. A need may be that which is wanting in general terms, or what is required to perform a particular job. There are overtones of the needy and deprived, which may or may not be intended. Perception of need may be induced: the marketing and selling of goods, for example, may depend on creating needs as well as meeting them.

If we are talking of the needs of teachers, we may be referring to basic essentials for minimum competent performance, or we may be referring to what is needed for teachers to provide the best possible service. Teachers' perceptions of need will relate to the work they now do, or to the gap between present circumstances and those which would enable them to work as they would wish. This is also true of others' perceptions of their need, particularly if it is hoped that teachers will perform a changing role. There are different categories of need, even within the 'professional' bracket. Training, retraining and development needs are not of the same order as the need for a sense of shared purpose and ethos, or the need for public understanding. The identification of need, bringing together subjective and external perceptions, relies at present on formal and informal appraisal systems, which are more likely to be focused on the job in hand, on the particular individual in relation to the particular school or service, and which are in any case patchily practised. Beyond the bread and butter negotiations for salaries and conditions of service, matters for employers, the union dimension of teacher associations and salary review board, the needs of teachers as a whole are not likely to be served or informed by the existing instruments.

Recognition

In the ways we use this word, there are at least two distinct elements, of identity and of appreciation (or the lack of either or both). The identity of teachers as a body has to do with the need of individual teachers to identify with each other, and to identify their individual work with that of teachers generally. It also has to do with a need to be accurately identified by the wider public. If the word 'teacher' is used, what does it suggest:

dedication, trustworthiness, learning, pedagogical skills; or in the plural, perhaps through media headlining, the word may equate more closely with discontent, short hours, disputes, the cause of economic decline and indiscipline. The image of the teacher is not that of teachers collectively. There is no collective body to reflect the distinctiveness of teaching as experienced by individual teachers, or to communicate with the public about the core of the teacher's identity and role, by which a teacher can be recognized.

Secondly, appreciation: in French, *reconnaissance* means also gratitude, acknowledgement; in German, *Anerkennung* is an extension of recognizing. By appreciation, we may mean gratitude and acknowledgement; or we may just mean having an understanding of what it is about. Both of these are needed by teachers in the public domain, just as they are by anyone else working for others. However, the word recognition may also be used by those wishing to withdraw it: 'I recognize the argument for this, BUT ...' In retrospect, this could have been the interpretation of a new Prime Minister's remarks in November 1992 about recognizing and wishing to enhance the status of teachers, as a prelude to taking yet more political and bureaucratic powers over their work. From surveys of public attitudes to teachers and schools, there appears to be a gulf between the high levels of parents' satisfaction with their own schools and teachers, and much lower opinions of schools and teachers generally at the macro-level, where populist press and politicians may intervene.

How can that gap be bridged?

Professional status

Status, or its near-synonym 'standing', is also used in different ways. It tends to be about place in society, and is used generally about high placing or the wish for it. A status symbol, for example, would probably not be about the underclass. There is a permanence about it. The word is linked to 'estate' (or in German *Stand*, French *état*), with the pre-democratic upper crusts of society. Professional status has that background, further developed since the nineteenth century. It is conferred on groups of people with highly trained skills and qualities founded on a recognizable body of knowledge and research, who take a large measure of responsibility for an essential service performed in the public interest. That responsibility is vested in a professional body with publicly recognized powers to determine what are the required levels of good practice and who is fit or unfit to exercise it. We could not describe philately as a profession: it may have highly trained skills and a recognizable body of knowledge, but it does not require a long period of high-level training beyond apprenticeship/experience, and above all, it would be difficult to argue that it performs an essential public service. These days, 'profession' is increasingly 'graduate profession', with a research base in a university-level discipline. For some, the word presents difficulties as being either outmoded or overused; for teachers in England and Wales, it has a particular force in terms of status, because in England and Wales they are the only major profession without such a professional body, and without powers to exercise their professional responsibilities collectively as well as individually. In other countries, professional status is not a necessary or even understandable notion, where teachers are part of the civil service structure, and aspects of their status relate to that.

Teachers

It has already been suggested that different feelings attach to teacher and its plural. This is not only true of the public perception, but has an effect on the commitment of any one teacher to colleagues in a school, and even more to the organized teaching body. What and who is a teacher? The obvious answer might be someone who is trained to teach and practises teaching. We then have different categories of teacher: beginning teachers, supply teachers, returning teachers, senior teachers and so forth, who may have very different needs. We may even be thinking of future teachers, and the circumstances in which potentially good teachers will be drawn to teaching or be deterred from it. Teachers of different specialisms may see themselves differently, and certainly there are different situations in different kinds of school and different areas. To address a general question about teachers, we have to look for the common factors.

But what about heads and deputies? Is the job of managing a school a teaching job? The question is not answered by demonstrating that the head *also* teaches; indeed, that suggests that the job of headship itself is not a part of teaching. There is by now, after many decades of separation, a sense of identity between primary and secondary school teachers in Britain, reflected by the fact that only one school teacher association remains confined to one sector. But does that extend to pre-school education, in its various forms? Does it extend to those whose work derives from an initial teaching qualification and experience, but who do not work in schools: advisers, education officers, teacher-trainers or educational psychologists? What of teachers in further and higher education? Are they teachers or lecturers; are they felt by themselves, by teachers in schools and by students and the public to be in the same continuum of public service? Is research a part of teachers' professional practice, either a part in which all teachers are engaged directly or a part in which some teachers depend on others for a specialized activity?

If the answer to all of these questions is affirmative, there is scope for considering teaching as a profession. If not, further credence is given to those who see teaching for different reasons as a sub-profession, although it has to be said that their reasons applied to other accepted professional groups would reduce them even more. It could well be argued that for teachers to gain status and professional recognition, they would have to see themselves and be seen as the whole education service, including the training, researching, managing and developing that informs teaching itself. It is of course difficult for some of the subgroups to avoid the temptation to seek their own higher status as specific professional groups, as for example educational psychologists, heads, academics and education officers, or even special educators.

The argument of this chapter is that all these specific groups are teachers, and that there is a shared professional responsibility and commitment to each other.

CONFIDENCE, TRUST AND MORALE

Professional needs are closely related to questions of motivation and morale. In 1990, the House of Commons Committee for Education, Science and the Arts (ESAC, 1990) noted with concern the contrast between the Houghton Report (1974) assertion that 'after the family, the teacher is the most important influence on the next generation' and the statement from Her Majesty's Inspectorate that many teachers 'feel their profession and its work are misjudged and seriously undervalued.' It therefore sought ways to improve the morale of the profession, and one of its principal recommendations (the one not to be adopted by the government of the day) was the creation of a General Teaching Council for England and Wales (Scotland's GTC was established in the 1960s). 'We believe that the positive effect on morale from a properly constituted and effective council warrant such effort.'

Generalizations about morale across well over half a million teachers are difficult and dangerous, but the HMI and select committee statements were well founded, and there is little doubt that morale plummeted from the low point of the 1980s. In the 1993 Oxford Employment Life Survey (Gallie and White, 1993), teaching was found to be the most stressful of the professional occupations, along with social work. Part of the problem was beyond education: from the early 1970s, a weakening British economy requiring scapegoats, together with falling school rolls combined to lower the public priority given to education and to add to the difficulty of maintaining confidence. The industrial disputes of the mid-1980s were a symptom rather than a cause, but certainly did not improve either public confidence or teachers' confidence in themselves or each other. There may have been 'a deep professional and public commitment to an underlying unity of purpose (GTC, 1992), but there were times when coming to the surface and being visible might have been more to be desired than the depth of burial.

It has also to be said that high professional morale is not an end in itself. Rather it is to be seen as a prerequisite to the kind of public service which teaching aspires to offer and which at its best it provides. Moreover, the raising of morale is not usefully to be seen as strengthening the 'feel good' factor without attending to the underlying causes of disenchantment. So, for example, a General Teaching Council would not by itself raise morale and motivation. It would contribute to the conditions required to do so; with the GTC would come a sense of ownership which would have to be reflected also in management styles in schools, in which teachers would have a real influence on content and policy, be it in schools or in the nurture of their profession as a whole.

There has been some recognition that for recruitment purposes the image of teaching has to be positively projected. This was the job of the government unit TASC (Teaching as a Career), now transferred to the Teacher Training Agency 'quango' and centred in a 'promotion of teaching' working group. Such activities may improve or lower teacher morale: if serving teachers see full-page advertisements of the kind used to lure others into the army, and if the image being presented does not correspond to their reality, they will resent it and quite understandably conspire to correct the distortions. For as ESAC recognized, teachers are the main ambassadors for teaching. It is worthy of note that in Scotland, the corresponding agency is lodged with the General Teaching Council. Government responsibility for ensuring supply is not passed to the GTC; but it is recognized by the Scottish Office that partnership with the body elected by teachers to oversee professional quality is essential if the public image of teaching as a career is to be properly projected, both to those who might become teachers and to an approving body of existing teachers.

RECOGNITION OF THE TEACHING ROLE

In wanting public appreciation for their work, teachers are faced with a dilemma. They are exasperated and demoralized by the perception of teachers as having short hours and long holidays, whether it is expressed in the jovial bantering of neighbours or for their own purposes by the populist media or politicians. But there is also a professional satisfaction in concealing the necessary background preparation, administration and follow-up, and sharing only the direct transactions of teaching and learning. The reward of teaching is the achievement and fulfilment of learners, enabled by teachers but not owned by them. So the efforts they have made behind the scenes are not their first concern for praise. What teachers want appreciated and celebrated is first and foremost learning. In this they differ from some other professions. It would be difficult for a defending lawyer to celebrate the innocence of the client rather than the skill with which that verdict has been gained. The lawyer's prime concern is not a change or improvement in or by the client. In the medical profession, there are different emphases of professional satisfaction as between consultants, surgeons, family practitioners and nurses. The former will derive high professional satisfaction from the exercise of special skills; the latter will have a higher level of satisfaction in enabling patients to share and take over the business of recovering health.

Teaching, as portrayed recently by Meryl Thompson, has a distinctive blend of competence, care and commitment, all of which are essential to the professional ethic (Thompson, 1995). A sense of mission and purpose has been identified as a key factor in successful teaching. There have been some useful recent studies of what teachers actually do. These could serve as a factual account to the public, without teachers themselves having to justify themselves. Of particular interest is the study (Campbell and Neill, 1994a) in the Teaching as Work Project. It not only shows teachers as a whole working a 54-hour week in school term time, equivalent to 46 hours in a 48-hour week, but it also identifies the proportion of time spent on different essential tasks, and shows which of these, notably administrative tasks, have grown since the last such survey in the 1970s (Hilsum and Strong, 1978). It relates its findings also to recent surveys of teacher motivation and morale, such as that from the London School of Economics (Varlaam, Nuttall and Walker, 1992). This survey had shown incursions into teachers' time for normal living as a source of demotivation second only to the public portrayal in the media. My own work with young teachers suggests that for them it is even more keenly felt and needs much attention to be brought under control. These, however, are the 'invisibles' of the teaching craft, which teachers themselves are reluctant to expose to their pupils or parents.

Campbell and Neill address the particular question of 'conscientiousness' with some caution. Their work confirms that teachers on average spend about 11 hours more time than they consider to be reasonable; that on average they consider about 9.3 hours per week beyond the 33 hours of directed time to be reasonable; and that those who most exceed such time are those for whom the level of non-directed time to be considered reasonable is highest. On the one hand, it may be considered to be 'professional' to be devoting such extra time to the job; on the other hand, it could be considered in other professions to be a sign of incompetence or exploitation, to be discouraged or to be countered with skills in the control of time. Looked at this way, would it be desirable for the public to know how such additional time is devoted to work? Or is it professional to have taken on additional responsibilities for child-minding, health and social care which may not be directly related to teaching and learning?

It is a question which arises again with the recent populist political initiative to promote sports in schools by using the national lottery, which may be compared for its peculiarly English equivocation to the profits made by the Church Commissioners from Sunday openings of their superstore complex in Gateshead. Although there are no satisfactory national statistics to demonstrate it, there is no doubt among those who work in schools that the other pressures on teachers' non-directed time, together with the decline in morale and school resources, have had the most damaging effects on extracurricular activities, notable in sports and the arts. The recent study (West and Perritt, 1995) across London schools demonstrates this clearly. For a politician to throw punters' money at the problem without any consideration of the key role of teachers and the use of their time is to be seen as an absurdity, and certainly the last kind of 'special offer' which will raise morale or motivation, even though the offer will no doubt be accepted by teachers clutching at straws, along with all the additional strains it will bring.

RESPONSIBILITY AND ACCOUNTABILITY

The accountability of teachers is complex and multiple. It may be, for example, to the employer, to the client (whether student or parent), to the local community, to 'society', to the next stage of education or employment for which education is preparing, to the teacher's own principles, to other teachers, whether in a line of responsibility or to the teaching profession as a whole, to the disciplines which teachers profess. It may be possible for divisions of responsibility to be made, so that at least prime responsibility in one or other or these directions is recognizable. But there will always be a tension among them, and one key part of professional discretion is in the resolution of these tensions.

Halford (1994) has usefully distinguished six models of accountability, which he describes as central control, self-accounting, consumerist, chain of responsibility, professional and partnership, and gives an account of the strengths and weaknesses of each. His conclusion is that 'all forms of responsive accountability work best in situations of trust where there is broad agreement on fundamental values.' He looks for 'a sufficient basis of shared values to enable all the world views represented within our culturally diverse society to work together within a common educational system.'

There is no doubt that in the last decade, the emphasis has been on central control and consumerist models, which might be thought to contradict each other but are in practice complementary. From the nineteenth-century heritage of loose government controls and professional élites which were legitimized for virtually all professions other than teaching came the assertion of a Secretary of State in the 1970s (Mulley, 1975) that his only direct powers to intervene in schools were to authorize the removal from their premises of derelict air-raid shelters. This was still the context of the 10/65 circular to promote the government policy of comprehensive schools, which was not and could not have been a directive. There was a division of powers between the state, local government and 'the schools', which in practice meant professional associations, over resource distribution, the content of education and the way it was organized. This was a situation in which teachers were able to exercise professional initiatives and judgements, to have space and responsibility for their work, even while remaining a disorganized profession. Vernon Bogdanor (1979) was able to record that

> Power was ... diffused amongst the different elements and no one of them was to be given a controlling voice ... For parallel to the formal relationships between central and local government, embodied in statute and convention, there grew up a network of professional communities whose role it was to soften the political antagonisms which might otherwise render the system unworkable ... the diffused structure of decision-making led, it could be argued, to better decisions because it ensured a wide basis of agreement before changes were made.

By 1976, however, central government intervention was being pressed from Downing Street on the Department of Education and Science. Since 1979, first a set of consumerist 'choice' measures were imposed, and then they were made the servant of central government regulation. The resultant pattern has been of the kind previously more associated with Central and East European régimes, although it has to be said that such régimes usually ensured that there was educational expertise among their ministers, whereas the assumption of powers in Britain has been accompanied by the dismissal from the ministry building of anyone to do with the 'educational establishment' or of any body such as Her Majesty's Inspectorate, appointed by the Crown, which might articulate an educational view of policy. All consultative representative advisory bodies were eliminated by 1985. Within the space of a few years, central government took powers to direct funds for in-service training, to control curriculum and examinations, salaries and conditions of service, and teacher training. It successfully provoked teacher associations to debilitating industrial action. It eroded drastically the powers of local authorities. In doing so, it weakened not only local democracy but the role of leading professional educators, since local authorities were required to have education committees and professional officers. The consumerism consisted of encouraging parents both to choose schools and to control them according to the regulations and standards laid down and publicized by government. Governors and parents were to become government agents and informants. The word 'teacher' is all but banished from the Parent's Charter. All this is well known to teachers of the time, and many commentaries are licking wounds, for there is no doubt that teachers have been deeply wounded. The fact that things have not worked the way the legislation has pointed is a tribute to the partnership between parents and teachers, based on their shared prime concern for the welfare of children. As Campbell and Neill (1994) have concluded, 'the occupational culture of the school remained stubbornly at odds with the assumptions of central government legislation on working conditions, and especially with the intended impact of performance-related pay.'

These new directions have affected other services and other professions, too. But of the major professions only teaching (in England and Wales) has been without a statutory professional council able to exercise proper influence on the quality of service to be expected. Even nursing secured an enhanced and unifying professional council in 1983, with funding and responsibility for nurse training being transferred from the Department of Health to a national board for the profession. Nurses, moreover, have always retained strong public sympathy and could not be assailed by the media. It was the lack of any such statutory body together with the conflicts among the several teacher unions which rendered teachers and schools particularly vulnerable to media exposure and political dogma when consensus politics were replaced by ideology. Whilst the change of political context may be seen to have been inimical to recognition of teachers' professional standing, it may also have contributed to the shared professional will to insist on it. For the one goal for which all professional teacher groups came together and stayed together through this destabilizing and debilitating period was the creation of a General Teaching Council.

PROFESSIONAL STATUS FOR THE FUTURE

Perhaps because of the lack of professional focus or an established body, there has been much useful re-exploration of teaching as a profession, in the radically changed context. Recent re-conceptualization is both an advance on traditional formulations of what constitutes a profession and suggests a model for the twenty-first century not confined to the traditions of one country. In contrast to the traditionally closed professions of élite minorities seen by Shaw as a conspiracy against the public, there have been the valuable explorations of 'the extended professional' by Hoyle (1975), the distinction between professionality and professionalism by Sockett (1980) and the articulation of 'open professionality' (Sayer, 1989) in the current proposals for a General Teaching Council. These, within the framework of the 'reflective practitioner', have been contrasted to the perceived deprofessionalization, de-skilling and proletarianization of teachers (Lawn and Ozga, 1988), in the technicist treatment of their work projected through legislation and management procedures. The traditional model of the teacher as an independent professional with a high degree of classroom autonomy has been modified to recognize that all teachers have responsibility for the teaching context and organization in which they practise. On the other hand, there are the warnings against 'contrived collegiality' (Hargreaves, 1991) and the insistence on teachers having genuine 'content participation' (Busher and Saran, 1992).

With these perceptions in mind, we have both to build on the general formulations of what constitutes a profession and to modify them. Characteristics generally identified as essential to a profession are:

a. that it performs an essential public service;
b. that its practice is founded on a distinctive body of knowledge and research;
c. that its members therefore undergo a lengthy period of initial education and training both in mastering that knowledge and in developing skills to execute it;
d. that this initial acquisition of knowledge and skill is complemented by continuing professional growth and development;
e. that it exercises a high degree of responsibility for the way it fulfils the objectives formed by the community of which it is a part;
f. that its members act with integrity and conscience primarily in the interests of their clients;
g. that its members accept and are governed by a code of ethics underwritten by its organization;
h. that it is well organized with disciplinary powers to enforce ethical practice;
i. that careful control is exercised over entry, training, certification and standards of practice.

Teaching, seen as a whole education service, corresponds to most of these criteria. It has a distinctive knowledge and skills base; it provides an essential service with integrity, in the interests of learners, and if necessary resists demands which are not in their interests. It has graduate preparation, despite the attempts of government to undermine that. Teachers are generally committed to reflecting on practice, improving and updating their skills.

Teachers need to feel responsibility for what they are doing. They need to have professional scope and space, to educate according to trained insights into students' learning. They need to assimilate, develop or create and have ownership of the teaching task. They need to feel responsible and professionally accountable for the quality of service provided for the public, and to be able to safeguard those they teach.

For that to be publicly recognized, the one most serious weakness at the moment, from which other weaknesses may be seen to derive, is the absence of a professional governing body with authority to articulate and exercise professional standards. At present some of the functions of a professional council are divided between a government department and a government-appointed agency. The weaknesses of such arrangements are outlined in the GTC proposals (GTC, 1995), from which parts of this chapter are drawn.

It is professionally unacceptable that a government department should administer decisions relating to professional competence or personal fitness to teach, without professional supervision. This applies both to the issuing of certificates entitling people to teach in schools and to the application of discipline relating to conduct. In no other profession are such professional matters in the hands of civil servants under political authority.

Moreover, there is no explicit code of ethics or understanding of the professional conduct expected of teachers by which such judgements can be properly exercised, and there cannot be without a fully representative body with the authority to develop such an understanding. Individual professional associations and institutions may contribute guidelines and exert their influence on members to follow them, but there is no adequate consensus and such voluntary disciplines have no force in law, and no direct bearing on decisions relating to fitness to teach and the protection of the public.

It is equally unsatisfactory that a government department or a government-appointed agency should make decisions on questions about the training and professional development of teachers, without having the advice of a competent body representing all aspects of these questions. By advice is meant formal advice requiring a response and requiring ministers to be answerable in Parliament if they have reason not to follow that advice. Consultation with individual bodies, whether seriously undertaken or a form of 'contrived collegiality' is no substitute for this. It is inappropriate that a government-appointed agency should represent to the public what is the nature of a career in teaching without having the advice of a body which reflects the professional judgement of the whole of the education service.

Existing operations do not have within them a satisfactory capacity for review, improvement of standards or development of good practice. The government was able previously to have regard to the advice of the Advisory Council on the Supply and Education of Teachers (ACSET), in moves towards a graduate or graduate equivalent schoolteaching profession, in extending the requirement of professional training for all maintained schools and in requiring professional training together with recent, relevant and substantial teaching experience for those charged with the professional aspects of initial training programmes for teachers. It is now in the position of making decisions without the joint advice and therefore commitment of those who must be depended on to implement them. After 1984 there remained no representative professional body to give such advice, and the politically appointed Council for the Accreditation of Teacher Education lacked professional support. The Council's remit has now transferred to the Teacher Training Agency, which is seen to suffer from the same disadvantage. It is essential that much of its work should be established as soon as possible within the general framework of a statutory professional council, related to the full range of professional concerns.

A further unsatisfactory element of present practice relates to recognition of teaching qualifications awarded outside the United Kingdom, and in particular the absence of an acceptable competent body to regulate and promote professional mobility between England and Wales and other member states of the European Union, which may now be expected to be an increasingly prominent feature of professional experience and aspiration.

This is not to criticize good work done by such government officials or agency executives; it is the absence of a whole-profession body which is the problem. However technically proficient such operations may be, they cannot be carried out satisfactorily without teachers taking a large measure of corporate responsibility for them. These are not functions which can be carried out *for* teachers or done *to* them, without diminishing their sense of professional responsibility. At present, then, teachers feel professionally responsible without having the recognized body which can regulate that responsibility.

The education service has had many divisions. There is, however, a deep professional commitment to an underlying unity of purpose, and there is an urgent need felt across the profession and supported by parents to establish a single recognized body with the authority to regulate and articulate those high professional standards and aspirations which will promote a teaching service of quality for future generations.

WHAT NEEDS WILL BE MET BY A GTC?

It has already been argued (Maclure, 1994) by supporters of the proposal that a General Teaching Council will not in itself be a panacea. It will symbolize professional self-esteem and provide a framework for professional service improvement. Like its counterpart in Scotland, it will establish and maintain a register of qualified teachers; it will oversee standards of entry to the profession; it will assert professional standards of conduct and exercise disciplinary powers to ensure they are maintained; it will have the responsibility to advise on the supply of teachers, and on their training and qualifications; it will establish the criteria by which courses of teacher training should be accredited; and it will provide the apolitical voice of the teaching profession as a whole.

It will not become involved in questions of remuneration or conditions of service, which are employment matters. It is not envisaged that it will have a direct role in curriculum policy, although it could well, as in Scotland, exert its influence to ensure that teachers are qualified to teach the specialisms and age-range for which they are employed, and therefore not expected to teach outside their trained capacities.

Among professional needs not at present being adequately met are:

a. *The induction of teachers*

A General Teaching Council should have the responsibility of promoting and disseminating good practice in induction in all parts of the education service, and could play a positive role in keeping under review and improving the quality of the professional development aspects of appraisal.

b. *Continuing professional development*

Whilst the concerns of the Teacher Training Agency for this area are welcome, the time is right for the General Teaching Council to assume both the advisory responsibilities which by now would include an advisory contribution to the establishment of national priorities, and also the wider functions of developing criteria, promoting good practice and recommending developments which would lead to greater consistency of opportunity and expectation in whatever part of the education service a teacher happens to be employed.

c. *Management training*

The Teacher Training Agency, having accepted a brief to develop the government 'Headlamp' initiative for newly appointed headteachers, should have the support and professional credibility of a General Teaching Council in this work.

d. *The supply, recruitment and retention of teachers*

There has been serious unevenness in recent years in the recruitment of teachers, and difficulty in predicting future trends. The recent economic recession has reduced graduate opportunities in other careers and has brought an increase of applications for courses of initial teacher training. This is however no prescription for the future. Indeed, an even more serious problem has been that the average length of a career in teaching, which had previously been increasing, has in the last few years declined, and once the economy moves out of recession, the retention and re-entry of teachers will be as great a challenge as initial recruitment. It is in the interests of any government in power and in the interests of the public that decisions about teacher supply and intake to courses of initial training, whether taken directly or through an appointed agency, should be informed by the considered and corporate advice of all parts of the education service, including employers, those who provide schools and training institutions. The General Teaching Council should have that advisory function. Fidler *et al.* (1993, p. 191) in making a thoughtful study of this problem conclude that:

> A professional, representative and broadly-based group is needed to oversee and coordinate the supply, recruitment, induction and in-service development of teachers. Such a body could air concerns and see that they were properly investigated. As Keep (1992) has pointed out, in other public services there is a clear national focus for personnel issues. Without such an intermediate body between central government and the schools, it is not clear where the focus is for professional management of the teaching force.

e. *Publication of information*

The General Teaching Council should be in a position to advise on good practice in professional education and training generally, and to be a source of information through commissioned study, publication and dissemination. The role as professional voice as portrayed in Scotland by Sutherland (1992) is even more necessary in the more tangled environment south of the Border:

The General Teaching Council is the voice of the teaching profession in Scotland. If the Council did not exist, it is difficult to know who would otherwise speak for the profession. The unions cannot speak for the profession with authority and credibility because
a   they cannot reflect the views of the whole profession
b   they are often in disagreement with each other on fundamental issues
c   they are increasingly political (a professional Council should be apolitical).
Since registration is a statutory requirement (as it must be if it is to be an effective control of standards) the Council is the only body which can give a view for all teachers in all sectors of the service.

BACKGROUNDS TO THE CURRENT GTC INITIATIVE

The attempts over nearly a century and a half to establish self-regulation for the teaching profession have been charted elsewhere, and are summarized in the GTC proposals (GTC, 1992; 1995). It is an accident of history that a GTC was not established in England and Wales at the same time as in Scotland, where the Committee chaired by Lord Wheatley recommended in 1963 'that there should be established a General Teaching Council for Scotland broadly similar in scope, powers and functions to the Councils in other professions.' Legislation for Scotland ensued in 1965, the Council being established in the following year.

In 1968, the incoming Secretary of State, Edward Short (now Lord Glenamara), announced his intention to establish a General Teaching Council and established a working party chaired by (Sir) Toby Weaver, with all the teachers' unions and associations, universities and teacher-trainers, local education authorities and the Department of Education. It has taken over a quarter of a century before another Secretary of State was appointed with personal experience and knowledge of the teaching role.

The current GTC initiative took up in 1983 the quiet work done among teacher associations in the late 1970s and the CATEC initiative of the College of Preceptors. By 1988, a detailed consultative document had been agreed by the 17 major associations involved, and has now been adopted by 30 of the bodies envisaged as initiating a statutory council. The Forum of these 30 associations, including teachers from all sectors, local authorities, parents, providers of institutions and governors, became a registered company limited by guarantee which now seeks to secure legislation for its statutory successor. It is partnered by a Charitable Trust which seeks to foreshadow the kind of advices and guidances which might be expected from the intended body, and which has produced or commissioned key preparatory consultative documents on the continuum of teacher education and training (GTC, 1992a; 1993; 1993a) and on ethical practice (Thompson, 1995).

NEW FEATURES IN THE GTC PROPOSAL

The first concern of the Council must be to safeguard the public as learners and clients in general and young people required to attend schools in particular. A second concern is that teachers should be able to exercise a large measure of responsibility for the standards and quality of the whole professional service they provide for the public. These concerns are reflected in the composition of the GTC (England and Wales) and the proposed composition of the statutory body. Teachers are seen to be those providing education in all sectors of the service: primary, secondary, further and higher education, maintained and non-maintained, heads and principals, teacher-trainers, education officers, psychologists, advisers and inspectors. Whilst the immediate first steps of the Council will be to establish a register of all those persons fit to teach in schools, the long-term aim is to extend such a function to the whole service, and the initial composition should reflect that aim. Secondly, whilst teachers must have a majority in the Council reflecting the responsibility for an appropriate measure of self-regulation, there is to be adequate representation from parents, governors, employment interests, providers in institutions and local and central government.

Two principles are established in this way. First, it is the whole of the education service which contributes to and accepts the disciplines of a professional body. Education is a service in which there is mobility across sectors of the service. For the health service, there is a division between doctors' and nurses' councils, and for the legal profession between solicitors and barristers. Teachers want no such hierarchies in education. Secondly, GTC tries to represent a new kind of 'open professionality' in which parents and others involved are seen as partners or co-educators, not merely as clients or consumers. Neither of these two elements was present in the 1965 constitution for the General Teaching Council for Scotland.

These proposals allow for the blend of self-accounting, professional, partnership, chain of responsibility and consumerist modes of accountability which Halford (1994) examined. They accommodate the 'extended professional' view of teachers as not just individual practitioners. They recognize the task of teaching not only to teach but to relate classroom practice to the internal school context and profession as a whole, and to the external environment.

FUTURE PROFESSIONAL NEEDS OF TEACHERS

Teachers as a profession will need to think ahead and formulate the professional requirements for future policy developments. There is a queue of obvious examples. The political will to extend nursery education will depend on the development of agreed training, standards and good practice. There is growing public awareness of the importance of standards of teaching in further and higher education generally, without adequate systems to recommend, initiate and develop good practice. Further decisions are required about the training and professional development of teachers in further and higher education. New forms of institutions and frameworks have been developing, particularly for the 16–19 age-group and community education, which combine elements associated with school and further education systems. Open learning, distance learning and the best use of new information technologies may be expected to become as important as institution-bound practice. A General Teaching Council reaching across the whole education service would be the appropriate body to promote research and advise on all of these and at the appropriate time to regulate practice.

Competence

The public interest in levels of competence among teachers is threefold: first, there must be a minimum level of competence against criteria agreed to be essential; secondly, this must be at least maintained and if necessary renewed; thirdly, skills and competencies of teachers must be developed to the highest potential in the interests of good learning. All three elements of the public interest should be promoted in all sectors and at all levels of the education service by the advice of the General Teaching Council and the active support of its members, combined with appropriate provision of training opportunity.

The check-lists of teaching competencies which have appeared in the last few years are likely to be the beginning of an approach to quality care which will extend across all occupations and across national frontiers. It is important that they should be given thorough professional scrutiny, and that the approach they represent should be neither overemphasized in relation to other approaches to teaching qualities, nor dismissed simply because the first formulations are so inadequate or have been so hastily applied by government agencies under political pressure.

The General Teaching Council should be expected to recommend to the Secretary of State what should be the stages of training and development through which competencies and levels of competence should be developed. This will also involve recommendations of both the entitlement of teachers, wherever they are employed, and the expectations on teachers to develop to the full their skills in the public service.

These responsibilities of the Council should extend to the recognition of qualifications and training received outside England and Wales; the Council should therefore include or be in a position to advise the lead body recognized as competent for that purpose, particularly in promoting professional mobility in the European Union and addressing the applicability of National Vocational Qualifications to teaching.

A lead body for further education has already been promoted by the Department of Employment, and may be expected to be pursued in the new Department of Education and Training. It must be either informed by the reflections of the whole teaching profession or be a part of its governing council.

The needs of a mobile teaching profession in Europe

Competencies may well involve certain approaches and attitudes conducive to the kind of society for which schools and colleges are to help learners to prepare. In addition to the obvious criteria of effectiveness, there are expectations in the national and international contexts of the widening European Union, including preparation for the exercise of democracy and human rights, and the will to promote active participation in this wider context. The new inclusion of school education and teachers' continuing development in programmes funded by the European Union has not just curricular but professional dimensions. European networks of training institutions have already been working together on European dimensions of teacher training. It is essential that the whole teaching profession becomes involved in such developments, and a General Teaching Council should be expected to be both an appropriate part of such networking and the body to relate these developments to internal professional expectations.

The status of teachers in the different member countries of the European Union will also be increasingly compared and examined for common elements. It is not at all clear whether the civil service status (and restriction) of teachers in some of the other member countries will be maintained. There are strong moves towards a GTC for the Republic of Ireland (INTO, 1994), and such new bodies as the Flemish Education Council have had a felt effect on the ability of teachers to share in determining their service to the community, and links with them will provide professional enhancement to the education service as it gradually grows into the European dimension.

Teachers and the public in this country need to be engaged in the general trends identified in Europe, beyond local and temporary ideologies. These include, as summarized by Bryan Peck (1992), an increasing emphasis on in-service training; attention to the beginning teacher and beginning headteacher; closer attention to entry requirements and selection of teachers; upgrading of teacher education courses; closer relationships between training institutions and universities; and a common concern to relate theory and practice.

CONCLUSION

This chapter has ranged discursively across the needs of teachers for recognition and professional status, accepting that needs may be both perceived by existing teachers and perceived by the society they serve. Because the education service is society's mainspring for the future, there lies behind the arguments advanced the fundamental question: what kind of society founded on what kind of values do we seek? The answer offered is to enable such a question constantly to be addressed and reinterpreted for practice, in a body of 'open professionality' which represents all teachers and those concerned with education, contributing to a learning society, and in a focused example joining in a 'community of educated persons'. Teachers need that shared sense of purpose. As Richard Pring (1995, p.195) reminds us,

> Teachers, with proper support and with the richness of various forms of cultural achievement as their resource, are capable of engaging in that transaction with young people ... But this is possible only if we constantly remind ourselves of the ethical base of our educational plans and purposes; otherwise 'education' is reduced to impersonal knowledge, coverage of curriculum content, the achievement of other people's objectives, inert ideas.
>
> To ensure that these moral questions are not suppressed by those, including government, who wish to subvert education to their own political or vocational ends, the ideals of this more generous concept of liberal education need to be preserved within a 'community of educated persons'. Such a community includes academics, artists, writers, scientists certainly who maintain and advance those cultural resources upon which teaching must draw. But it includes, too, members of the community, including employers, who quite rightly question the relevance of those resources to the economic and social world in which young people need to earn a living and find a quality of life. Above all, it includes teachers who mediate the inherited culture to the personal aspirations and needs of young people – who ensure that, whatever the differences in cleverness or good fortune or background amongst those young people, their common humanity is recognised and their capacity 'to become human' is enhanced.

REFERENCES

Bogdanor, V. (1979) 'Power and participation.' *Oxford Review of Education*, **5** (2), 157–68.

Busher, H. and Saran, R. (1992) 'Changing professional roles of teachers in the UK.' Conference paper: BEMAS, Bristol.

Campbell, R. J. and Neill S. R. St.J. (1994) *Primary Teachers at Work*. London: Routledge.

Campbell, R. J. and Neill S. R. St.J. (1994a) *Secondary Teachers at Work*. London: Routledge.

Education Science and Arts Committee (ESAC), House of Commons (1990) *The Supply of Teachers for the 1990s*. London: HMSO.

Fidler, B. *et al.* (1993) *The Supply and Recruitment of School Teachers*. London: Longman.

Gallie, D. and White, M. (1993) *Employee Commitment and the Skills Revolution: Findings from the Employment in Britain Survey*. Oxford: Nuffield College.

GTC (England and Wales) (1992) *Proposals for a Statutory General Teaching Council for England and Wales*. London: GTC.

GTC (England and Wales) (1992a) *The Induction of Newly Appointed Teachers: Recommendations for Good Practice*. Slough: NFER.

GTC (England and Wales) (1993) *The Initial Education and Training of Teachers: GTC Advices and Comments*. London: GTC.

GTC (England and Wales) (1993a) *The Continuing Professional Development of Teachers, with Recommendations for Good Practice*. London: GTC.

GTC (England and Wales) (1995) *Revised Proposals for a Statutory General Teaching Council for England and Wales*. London: GTC.

Hargreaves, A. (1991) 'Contrived collegiality: the micropolitics of teacher collaboration.' In Blase, J. (ed.) *The Politics of Life in Schools: Power, Conflict and Cooperation*. London: Sage.

Halford, M. (1994) 'Accountability and values.' In D. Scott (ed.) *Accountability and Control in Educational Settings*. London: Cassell.

Hilsum, S. and Strong, C. (1978) *The Secondary Teacher's Day*. Slough: NFER.

Houghton Report (1974) *Report of the Committee of Enquiry over the Pay of Non-University Teachers*. Cmnd.5848. London: HMSO.

Hoyle, E. (1975) 'Professionality, professionalism and control.' In Houghton *et al.* (eds) *Management in Education*, **1**. London: Ward Lock.

Irish National Teachers' Organization (INTO) (1994) *Comhairle Múinteoireachta: A Teaching Council – Accessible, Accountable, Autonomous*. Dublin: INTO.

Keep, E. (1992) 'The need for a revised management system for the teaching profession.' NCE Briefing Paper, published in 1993. *Briefings for the Paul Hamlyn Foundation National Commission on Education*. London: Heinemann.

Lawn, M. And Ozga, J. (1988) 'The educational worker? A re-assessment of teachers.' In J. Ozga (ed.) *Schoolwork*. Milton Keynes: Open University Press.

Maclure, S. (1993) 'A General Teaching Council for England and Wales?' In *Briefings for the Paul Hamlyn Foundation National Commission on Education*. London: Heinemann.

Mulley, F. (1975) Speech to the Headmasters' Association Annual Conference.

Peck, B. (1992) 'An education profession for tomorrow: the European dimension.' Conference paper: BEMAS, Bristol.

Pring, R. (1995) *Closing the Gap. Liberal Education and Vocational Preparation*. London: Hodder & Stoughton.

Sayer, J. (1989) *Towards The General Teaching Council*. London: Education Management Unit.

Sockett, H. (1980) 'Accountability: the contemporary issues.' In H. Sockett (ed.) *Accountability in the English Education System*. London: Hodder & Stoughton.

Sutherland, D. I. (1992) 'The Scottish experience of a General Teaching Council.' Conference paper: BEMAS, Bristol.

Thompson, M. (1995) *Professional Ethics and the Teacher*. London: GTC.

Varlaam, A., Nuttall, D. and Walker, A. (1992) *What Makes Teachers Tick? A Survey of Teacher Morale and Motivation*. London: London School of Economics.

West, A. and Perritt, H. (1995) 'Survey of inner London headteachers: educational expenditure and out-of-school and extra-curricular activities.' *Educational Research*, **37** (2), 159–76.

Chapter 3

The Career Structure and Remuneration of Teachers: A Headteacher's Viewpoint

Anne Waterhouse

Ask teachers anywhere why they choose to teach and the vast majority will reply they are committed to working with children and young people. At interview for initial teacher education courses applicants do not generally talk about salary structures but invariably refer to wanting to work with children. Yet there is still a public misconception that teachers, especially those working with young children, are little more than child-minders with convenient daily hours and long holidays. There remains a view that teachers have exceptional job security and considerable autonomy and that it is virtually impossible to sack a bad one. Many of these views are compounded by the current political climate with its populist crusade to improve standards. Allegedly trendy teachers and supposedly declining standards are blamed for many of the ills of society. Teachers are used as scapegoats for the perceived failures of imposed policies arising from increased central control over the work of schools and the academic performance of their pupils. The tensions between different functions that schools fulfil are rarely acknowledged by politicians neither is proper consideration given to the implications for the education service of the changing needs of society.

Concerns are growing over the process of deprofessionalization as conflicting tensions arise from the delegation of powers to governing bodies of schools, coupled with increased central government control over education. A downward spiral of teachers' morale and motivation is exacerbated by constant criticisms based on flawed political and ideological arguments. This development is accompanied by a legislative programme marked by a rapid pace of imposed change and by initiatives which are designed to have a major impact upon teachers' career development and related needs.

Teachers' daily working lives are spent within the confines of a particular institution and with meeting its aims. At the same time, considering the needs of individual pupils, and developing strategies to meet those needs, is the prime occupation of teachers. In theory, institutional aims should be based on the needs of pupils. In practice, as education services face draconian funding cuts, schools are forced into efficiency savings and made to participate in the competition of the market-place. Teachers are at the forefront of these tensions and the time for a realistic appraisal of their needs, in terms of a clearly defined career structure and equitable pay levels matched with professional conditions of service, has never been more necessary. Unfortunately the debate frequently revolves around issues such as resourcing, affordability, standards and an apparent unwillingness to forget past positions or to seek a consensus view about what is needed to advance the situation. Ian Lawrence, writing about 'Power and Politics at the Department of Education and Science', is right to criticize politicians, although teachers need to consider the options carefully too:

> The appraisal of educational resourcing is often made more difficult by the apparent obscurity of the issues and problems surrounding it. The recognition that the changes in society which have taken place in the UK since 1945 might be reflected in the education system is a task that politicians tend to avoid.
>
> (Lawrence, 1992, p. 124)

Many teachers hold the view that teaching is no longer recognized as a profession. They believe that teachers have been reduced to the level of technicians. Until the summer of 1994, with the appointment of Sir Ron Dearing to undertake a review of the National Curriculum arrangements, teachers were not involved in consultations on matters related to their work and were given little or no ownership over policy-making for reform or school improvement. Although the Burnham Committee system for negotiating teachers' pay was in need of review, the replacement of collective negotiating rights with a Pay Review Body debased professionalism and further affected morale and motivation. Despite these constraints, compounded by the introduction of delegated funding, there remained a need for teachers to consider how traditional expectations could change to meet developing educational requirements for the twenty-first century.

Alongside the introduction of the policy of Local Management of Schools (LMS), which devolves funding to schools, the role of the LEA changed. Delegation gives governing bodies the responsibility to manage school budgets, although there remain clear LEA statutory duties. Schools have to purchase services, previously provided by LEAs, but with current levels of underfunding many of them are not able to buy in what is required, thereby increasing pressures on teachers as well as blurring career structures.

Teachers salaries make up 80 per cent of the average expenditure of schools, and governing bodies are forced to make decisions about whether to secure the services of experienced, but consequently more expensive teachers, or employ recently qualified staff who do not cost as much. This situation is exacerbated by the central government requirement for LEA formula funding to be based on average rather than actual salaries. It is, however, important to consider the practicalities of a scheme paying actual salaries when there are no agreed mechanisms to identify minimum staffing levels. Teachers have to acknowledge that a salary structure, paying yearly increments, makes a demand to pay actual salaries almost impossible to meet and negates the basis of formula funding. There are, therefore, real tensions between ensuring fair and equitable funding for schools and meeting teachers' needs. Currently governors have the responsibility of determining the salaries of the teachers they employ within the framework of the Teachers' Pay and Conditions Document which is subject to amendment each year.

The Education Reform Act established the possibility of schools opting out of local government control and becoming self-governing Grant-Maintained schools (GMS) following a ballot of parents. GMS governors have the option of applying to the Secretary of State to opt out further from nationally determined pay and conditions for teachers. The discretion over salaries by governors in both LEA and GM schools has serious implications for teachers' career progressions. Teachers believe these developments have affected career structures and eroded the expectation of appropriate and equitable rates of pay for similar work undertaken by individual teachers in different schools.

Certain basic principles are needed to underpin the development of professional rates of pay and provide a clear career structure. Notwithstanding the commitment of people who work as teachers, pay and conditions must be attractive enough to recruit, motivate and retain good staff. Remuneration needs to be equitable within the profession and relate well to that of other professions. The issue of comparability must not be underestimated. Structures have to be seen to be fair by those working within a profession and outside of it. The structures need to be transparent and none of the parties involved should forget the importance of accountability. In addition there must be appropriate conditions of service. Teachers' working conditions are also children's working conditions which is an important point and often neglected. Teachers need to be paid an appropriate salary with access to a coherent career structure related to the work and responsibilities they are undertaking rather than to the size of a school or to a concept of affordability.

THE HISTORICAL CONTEXT

Following the onset of strike action and the withdrawal of goodwill by teachers in the pay dispute which started during the spring of 1984, teachers were described by Lord Beloff writing in the *Daily Telegraph* as 'the enemy within' (Beloff, 1985, p. 18), thus fostering a political and public mind-set about supposedly militant unprofessional teachers which still lingers a decade later. The dispute ran through 1985 and into 1986 when an interim salary settlement and a negotiated agreement brought about an uneasy truce. Talks took place under the auspices of ACAS in relation to pay, conditions of service, negotiating machinery and appraisal which eventually led to final agreement.

It was in response to this agreement in the autumn of 1986 that the then Secretary of State, Kenneth Baker, introduced the Teachers' Pay and Conditions Bill which sought parliamentary approval for the removal of teachers' negotiating rights. The 1987 Pay and Conditions Act set down a new pay structure and a new definition of teachers' duties and directed working time. Directed Time was defined as 1265 hours over 195 days during which a headteacher could direct a teacher who, in addition, should

> work such additional hours as may be needed to enable him to discharge effectively his professional duties, including, in particular, the marking of pupils' work, the writing of reports on pupils and the preparation of lessons, teaching material and teaching programmes. The amount of time required for this purpose beyond the 1265 hours ... and the times outside the 1265 specified hours at which duties shall be performed shall not be defined by the employer but shall depend upon the work needed to discharge the teacher's duties.
>
> (DfE, 1995, para 40.7, p. 50)

Five days beyond the pupils' year of 190 days were identified for INSET and management-related activities. The document also separated the duties of heads and deputies from those of teachers.

The Pay and Conditions Act established an Interim Advisory Committee (IAC) to make recommendations for determining teachers' pay and conditions under the direction of the Secretary of State. The IAC was directed to look at the recruitment, retention and motivation of sufficient high quality teachers at national and local levels while being heavily constrained to consider the effects of affordability.

The Education (No. 2) Act of 1986 introduced new statutory responsibilities for governing bodies and gave the Secretary of State power to introduce teacher appraisal schemes. By the end of 1987 the government was heralding its Great Education Reform Bill which was enacted in July 1988. The Education Reform Act 1988 (ERA) was seen by teachers' organizations as one of the most retrograde pieces of educational legislation in the history of the country. It established an enabling framework for the education system but actual implementation required more detail which successive education acts put into place. As well as giving unprecedented powers to the Secretary of State, ERA reduced the role and power of Local Education Authorities and enhanced the responsibilities of individual school governing bodies with the transfer to them of discretionary powers.

Children became 'age-weighted pupil units' according to a formula, admissions to schools were subject to open enrolment and the delegation to governing bodies of the management of school budgets, shared with responsibilities for the appointment and dismissal of staff, impacted upon teachers' career and employment prospects within the national pay and conditions scheme. GMS governors could establish their own conditions and pay outside the prescribed pay and conditions order.

At the same time as the legislation began to impact upon schools, concerns about teacher supply into the 1990s were growing along with anxieties about the emergence of a demographic 'time bomb'. Although the government sought to convey the view that there was no general shortage of teachers there was an acknowledgement that there were problems in certain subject and geographical areas. The situation was examined by the House of Commons Select Committee for Education, Science and the Arts. The IAC was asked to consider the issue of teacher recruitment and retention and received information from a joint survey undertaken by the six teacher organizations. The survey identified the extent of shortage subjects with 53 per cent of teachers teaching subjects for which they had no post-A-level qualifications. The independent Institute of Manpower Studies produced a report on the supply of teachers, drawing attention to the increasingly competitive labour market for graduates and emphasizing the need for a major initiative in teacher recruitment and retention.

As early as 1984, Lord Vaizey, among others, had been urging the introduction of differentiated pay for mathematics and science teachers and discussing the use of performance-related pay (PRP) (Vaizey, 1984, pp. 50–1). The IAC report of February 1989 considered the effects of the ERA on the duties and responsibilities of all teachers but particularly on heads and deputies. It did not recommend different basic salaries for teachers in different subject areas and it rejected regional pay differentiation as inflexible and cost-ineffective although it did recommend the discretion to award accelerated increments.

With delegated funding school governors became responsible for deciding numbers of staff appropriate to their individual schools. Their powers relating to appointments and dismissals and the operation of disciplinary and grievance procedures saw many using temporary contracts to manage staffing budgets. Evidence indicated that general comparability prevailed between graduates at the beginning of careers but by the time those who had elected to teach were in their mid-career there was a growing gap with 'very poor pay prospects' (National Commission, 1993, p. 222).

In 1990 the IAC recorded the view that the majority of teachers would be worse off than during the previous year because of external economic circumstances. At this time there was an insufficient number and an inadequate level of incentive allowances for teachers in primary schools. The outcomes of joint surveys undertaken by the six teacher organizations indicated that teacher shortages affected the whole country and all subjects and age-groups. Problems over supply provision to cover teacher absence and mismatch were also indicated.

The third report of the IAC recommended a new higher level 'standard scale' and the introduction of local discretion to enhance increments, introducing the concept of local pay scales. As well as recommending increases to the five incentive allowance rates, the IAC suggested that more teachers should be eligible for these allowances. A common pay spine was introduced for heads and deputies as were other recommendations about supply cover and incremental progression for part-time teachers.

The fourth, and final, IAC report was published in January 1991. The remit for 1991–92 was limited by comparisons with the annual percentage movements in the pay of non-manual employees outside the public services sector, leading to a recommendation of 9.5 per cent. This was felt by the committee to be more acceptable, increasing teachers' morale and, when considered alongside proposed new negotiating machinery, was seen to be a positive development. Recruitment and retention difficulties still existed and the report perceived that LEAs and governing bodies taking account of local circumstances would be the most appropriate strategy for achieving increased non-contact time along with better targeting of INSET provision.

The proposed restoration of limited negotiating rights was contained in the 1990 Bill which was suddenly withdrawn and replaced with the second School Teachers' Pay and Conditions (No. 2) Bill. The IAC was replaced by a permanent School Teachers' Review Body (Busher and Saran, 1992, p. 20). Kenneth Clarke, as Secretary of State for Education, extolled the virtues of Review Bodies in delivering higher levels of pay and the majority of the teachers' organizations supported the proposal. Later, as Chancellor, Clarke stated the opposite, declaring that Review Bodies should not deliver relatively higher awards than the private sector.

The remit for the Review Body did not include any cash or percentage limits but introduced consideration of performance-related pay. As part of its submission to the Review Body the National Union of Teachers put forward a claim for improvements to teachers' conditions of service as well as a pay claim:

- mandatory national limits should be placed upon all class sizes;
- contractual limits should be placed on a teacher's obligation to cover;
- national entitlements to non-contact time should be introduced;
- a national induction scheme should apply to all new entrants;
- statutory entitlements to in-service training should be introduced;
- additional teacher support staff should be provided in all schools;
- limitations should be placed upon the working time of teachers.

(National Union of Teachers (1992), *Annual Report for 1992*, p. 99)

The new Review Body reported on the complexities of the pay structure and the need for simplification. Problems of recruitment and retention were seen to have diminished although it was acknowledged that there was likely to be some deterioration in the situation as the recession weakened. The Review Body warned about the dangers of complacency in relation to 'the mismatch between teachers' qualifications and how they are deployed' (STRB, 1992, para. 50, p. 10). In order to give flexibility to governing bodies managing individual school budgets, statutory limits on the numbers of deputy heads employed in schools were removed. Comments were made on the proportionately fewer numbers of incentive allowances available to primary school teachers with proposals to increase the numbers of the allowances available as from September 1992. The Review Body stated that PRP in teaching would not provide the basis for improved recruitment and retention which were dependent upon adequate basic pay levels.

New arrangements for inspecting schools were established following the Education (Schools) Act 1992. The Office for Standards in Education (OFSTED) took over many of the former duties and responsibilities of HMI. The Framework for the Inspection of Schools contained criteria which further influenced the need for teachers to have a coherent career and pay structure, with OFSTED supporting in principle a need for flexibility on the pay spine (Office of Manpower Economics, 1995, p. 5).

Alongside the legislative changes directly affecting teachers, continuing concerns about the quality of initial teacher training saw the development of government initiatives aimed at producing a growing involvement for schools. The DES had proposed the Licensed Teacher Scheme in 1988, introducing a non-standard route to qualified teacher status for overseas trained teachers and others. In 1989 the Articled Teacher Scheme, the forerunner of school-based training schemes, which was partly intended to meet concerns about teacher supply, was introduced. This positive programme was later abandoned because of its high costs. In 1992 the Secretary of State announced to the North of England Education Conference his intention to introduce school-based training schemes. The developments in School Centred Initial Training Schemes (SCITS) and partnership schemes with higher education institutions and colleges had implications for the professional development and career structures of serving teachers.

A White Paper, *Choice and Diversity*, was translated into the 1993 Education Act. One of the central provisions of the Act was to establish a Funding Agency for schools (FAS) to administer existing grant-maintained schools and to undertake, eventually, many of the strategic functions and responsibilities of LEAs. The Teacher Training Agency was established to control funding and entry to initial teacher education and to initiate research related to initial training. The first TTA corporate plan in March 1995, however, envisaged a widening remit to include a review of continuing professional development, the introduction of profiles for newly qualified teachers and a more rigorous approach to INSET and management training for headteachers.

Prior to the deliberations of the Pay Review Body for 1993–94, the Chancellor of the Exchequer announced central restrictions on public sector pay to a maximum of 1.5 per cent. The second STRB report noted that local authorities would have to seek efficiency savings, implying a consequent deterioration in staffing levels for individual schools. Recommendations for a single spine pay structure with additional points for qualifications, experience, responsibilities, excellence and recruitment and retention factors were adopted. The need to improve the management of schools was recognized and amendments to the professional duties of deputy heads in the Pay and Conditions Document were accepted. Induction for new teachers remained a priority and the Review Body registered its continuing concern. No recommendation over the virtual lack of non-contact time available for primary teachers was forthcoming.

By the time the third STRB report was published, in February 1994, the new pay spine had only been in operation for five months. The Review Body noted that although supply, recruitment and retention of primary teachers was not seen to be a particular problem there was not the same sense of reassurance about the position in secondary schools. It recorded a high level of professional commitment, although individual teachers' excessive workloads were having a detrimental effect. The salary level of returners to teaching was identified as an issue and the duties of headteachers were amended to include appropriate provision of support to new teachers and returners.

The fourth report of the Review Body, published in February 1995, continued to track important issues in the context of a proper career structure for teachers. The decline in the number of qualified full-time teachers and the growth in the employment of qualified part-time teachers were noted. Significant expansion of the employment of non-teaching support staff was reported. Unqualified support staff were invariably cheaper than qualified teachers. The introduction of LMS and a more flexible use of resources were identified as the main reasons for this. The volume of administration individual schools were required to undertake, because of the diminution of the role of LEA administration, could also account for the trend. Many teachers expressed concern over the changing staffing pattern, coinciding with severe budget cuts and a rise in class sizes, because of the predicted effects upon the provision of effective education for their pupils.

Again the STRB claimed there was no evidence to suggest recruitment and retention difficulties. Minimal problems in recruiting to initial teacher education were noted. Performance Related Pay indicators for heads and deputies were recommended for the guidance of governing bodies in conducting statutory annual pay reviews. There was little evidence that governing bodies were making use of excellence points although the STRB acknowledged the use of discretionary points to reward experience, additional responsibilities and recognition of degrees.

There was an acknowledgement of the previous concern about non-contact time in primary schools and a decline noted in its availability in secondary schools but no recommendation about establishing a statutory minimum entitlement was made. The Review Body's survey into workload showed heads and deputies working up to 61 hours and classroom teachers 55 hours in the average working week. Again the Review Body did not make recommendations about working hours or class size but commissioned a further survey. The Secretary of State proposed to accept, and implement from 1 September 1995, the Review Body's recommendations in relation to governing bodies' powers to compensate teachers for INSET undertaken at weekends and in school holidays, but would not sanction that existing discretion could be utilized to reward teachers who undertook duties in relation to school-based initial teacher training.

The STRB published a consultative document on possible modifications to the pay structure for classroom teachers in May 1995. The document sought comments on 'three broad ways to achieve greater flexibility'; to increase the number of smaller spine points; a change to the present additional points, including the removal of the equivalent to the current first 'special needs' point; or, the granting of power to governing bodies to 'award sums of any value between existing points'; and two alternative strategies for smoothing the pay spine (Office of Manpower Economics, 1995, pp. 7

and 10). In July 1995 the Review Body also consulted upon a further proposed survey of teachers' workloads in 1996 and whether or not the changes to the National Curriculum Tests had affected the need for such a follow-up.

THE ISSUES

Recruitment and retention

The Teacher Training Agency (TTA) was established in September 1994. Its first corporate plan was published in March 1995 and, amongst other aims, sought 'to ensure that the teaching profession attracts high-quality candidates in sufficient numbers to meet the needs of schools' by co-ordinating priorities including 'the promotion of teaching as a profession' (TTA, 1995, pp. 3, 2). The TTA commissioned a review of how teaching as a career should be promoted, which identified that teacher shortages remain across geographical and subject areas and noting that there should not be complacency about an apparent easing of recruitment into teaching because of the recession.

> Teaching will continue to face effective competition from other professions for high calibre entrants and the aim should be to establish effective marketing plans and mechanisms for delivery which will compare favourably with the best on offer elsewhere.
> (Wadsworth, 1995, para. 1.5)

As well as considering the future demand for teachers and recruitment for initial training, the position of re-entrants to the profession must also be considered. There needs to be a serious examination of the dramatic increase in the numbers of experienced teachers seeking early retirement and the numbers taking ill-health retirements.

Pay, motivation and career progression

The National Commission on Education identified that 'Career progression and rewards for experienced teachers are not sufficient to ensure recruitment, retention and motivation of high-quality professionals' (National Commission on Education, 1993, p. 221). The work undertaken by the National Commission identified a range of issues which need to be considered in a new structure for salaries and progression. These include 'competitive and flexible entry points' following an induction period, advance up the pay spine of at least two points after the award of qualified teacher status and strategies to motivate teachers (National Commission, 1993, p. 223).

An independent study funded by the University of Hertfordshire presented evidence from a survey undertaken in April to June 1994 to the STRB. The authors, Healy and Kraithman, warned of the dangers of believing that the Dearing approach to consultation for the National Curriculum would resolve all the concerns of teachers. They urged that the National Curriculum reforms and the consequent workload implications should be kept under review. The study indicated concerns of teachers relating to LMS and drew attention to evidence which suggest that younger, less experienced teachers are appointed by governing bodies for financial rather than educational reasons. Mobility appears to be constrained as more experienced teachers no longer feel able to seek to broaden their teaching experiences because they cost more than their young and inexperienced colleagues. Feelings of job insecurity are increasing for the same reasons:

> A very high proportion of teachers are affected by the bringing of market criteria into recruitment and selection of teachers and our study would suggest that primary school teachers feel more affected. This is not surprising since each primary school teacher's salary will be a very visible outgoing from the budget allowed to such a school. Experienced teachers now feel locked into their current jobs as they feel they will be too expensive to employ elsewhere.
>
> (Healy and Kraithman, 1994, para. 3.1.2, p. 9).

There are also problems with responsibility points. Healy and Kraithman urged that known objective criteria should be used in the allocation of points. Table 3.1 emphasizes a gender imbalance with men being awarded higher level responsibility points than women. The respondents to the survey expressed opposition to any scheme for Performance Related Pay, citing the lack of proper funding for PRP and possible demotivation as a result of governing bodies having the power to award discretionary points; 'to add further complications may be very unwise. In the current climate where teachers seek stability, PRP may be best avoided' (Healy and Kraithman, 1994, para. 6.4, p. 16).

Table 3.1 *Number of teachers with points awarded for the criteria of responsibility by gender*

Responsibility Points Awarded	Men	%	Women	%	TOTAL
0	72	18.1	232	32.4	304
1	70	17.6	205	28.6	275
2	109	27.4	169	23.6	278
3	53	13.3	65	9.1	118
4	62	15.6	29	4.1	91
5	26	6.5	10	1.4	36
TOTALS	392	35.6	710	64.4	1102

Source: Healy and Kraithman, 1994, para. 5.1, p. 13

Comparability

Advice from the National Union of Teachers to the STRB for 1995 clearly illustrated the failure to address the relative decline in teachers' pay since the Houghton Committee of Inquiry reported in 1974. The Union drew its statistics from the DES submission to the 1990 Select Committee, updated in line with teachers' and non-manual employees pay (Table 3.2). Further information compiled by the Union for negotiations over teachers' pay in former Sixth Form Colleges gives comparative information about average salaries for graduates in 1994 (see Table 3.3).

The demographic time bomb

In his address to the 1995 North of England Education Conference, Ted Wragg warned of 'a very severe crisis in recruiting teachers' (Wragg, 1995, p. 14). He reminded his audience of difficulties in the 1980s recruiting mathematics and science teachers and of

Table 3.2.   *The decline in teachers pay compared to average non-manual earnings*

	Teachers' Average Earnings (£)	Average Non-Manual Earnings (£)	Teachers' Pay as a Percentage of Non-Manual Earnings (£)
1974	3080	2260	137
1975	3780	2920	130
1976	4180	3510	119
1977	4410	3830	115
1978	4900	4290	114
1979	5380	4790	112
1980	7380	6010	123
1981	8030	6940	116
1982	8620	7580	114
1983	9120	8270	110
1984	9650	8950	108
1985	10,390	9600	108
1986	11,220	10,450	107
1987	13,100	11,300	116
1988	13,670	12,520	109
1989	14,730	13,770	107
1990*	15,760	15,150	104
1991*	17,310	16,250	107
1992*	19,060	17,400	110
1993*	19,175	18,240	105
1.4.94*	19,965	18,950	105
31.3.95*	19,965	19,660	101.6

Source: DES *Submission to Commons Select Committee 1989/90*
*Figures for 1990 to 1995 are estimates derived from teachers' paybill increases and median forecast increases in average non-manual earnings (IRS Pay and Benefits Bulletin, Aug. 1994) (NUT, 1994, p. 22)

Table 3.3.   *Salaries in teaching and other comparable professions*

A: Average Salaries in Graduate Professions during 1994		£
Solicitors	Partners	44,626
	Senior Assistants	31,191
General Practitioners	Target income	41,830
Computer Specialists	Systems Managers	37,221
	Operations Managers	32,810
Chemical Engineers	Males only	32,536
Actuaries	Consultancies	31,500
	Insurance Companies	27,317
Accountants	Senior Company Accountants	30,000
Personnel Specialists	Departmental Managers	30,295
	Senior Personnel Officers	26,199
Electrical Engineers	Public Sector	27,000
	Private Sector	27,900
Teachers in former	Spine Point 9	19,920
Sixth Form colleges	Spine Point 10	20,841
	Spine Point 11	22,071

Source: Salary surveys published in IDS Management Pay Review during 1994

B: Graduate Staring Salaries		1994 £	1995 £
All Graduates	AGR estimate	13,500	14,000
Teachers in former	good honours graduate	13,200	
Sixth Form Colleges	other graduate	11,682	

Source: AGR Annual Survey, January 1994 and January 1995; National Union of Teachers (1995) unpublished information

current difficulties in modern languages and English. He referred to the present situation in the context of LMS, graduate unemployment and teacher redundancies. The number of teachers who are likely to be retiring in the next few years, particularly the increasing numbers who are seeking early retirement, together with alternative and more attractive prospects for graduates following improvements in the economy, together with enhanced alternative employment opportunities for young teachers are, in Wragg's view, going to have a 'devastating effect' on teacher supply (Wragg, 1995, p. 14). He illustrated the problems ahead resulting from the class of degrees being achieved by intending teachers of mathematics, physics and chemistry. Students are best qualified in English, modern languages and history. The picture he painted was bleak.

NATIONAL PAY SCALES AND CAREER STRUCTURE

The previous sections have illustrated a range of common threads which have implications for the development of a coherent structure for teachers' pay and career progression. This book considering a range of teachers' needs is published during a period of severe financial constraints for the education service. There is much that needs to be done in relation to developing positive attitudes at all levels. Without serious work being undertaken to improve the overall climate surrounding education, the continuing decline in teachers' morale will have detrimental effects on the work of schools. No amount of political intervention or the introduction of lists of technical competencies will enhance the quality and effectiveness of teachers.

The development of proper pay levels has to be considered alongside the need for increased overall expenditure and investment in education. The importance of ownership on the motivation of staff means that a strategy to enable the reintroduction of some form of pay negotiations, albeit not a replication of the Burnham Committee, needs to be developed as one element in the revitalization of education.

The complex formula for the Standard Spending Assessment of Local Authorities, undertaken by the Department for the Environment rather than the Department for Education, results in children in different parts of the country being deemed as worth more or less than their peers. This is iniquitous, particularly when considered in the light of a centrally controlled National Curriculum intended to give all children, regardless of where they live, access to the same opportunities. The same principle ought to be applied to teachers' pay, positing a national scale and national conditions of service to be administered within equitably funded Local Education Authorities. This should apply to all schools, be as clear, coherent and transparent as possible and be based on stability of funding for schools.

Another of the mechanisms which needs to be considered is the current DfE requirement for Local Authorities to delegate formula funding to individual schools. Any new model of delegation changing from the basis of average salaries would require corresponding changes to salary structures, with the possible removal of the expectation of automatic annual increments. However, without change of some sort it is going to become increasingly difficult for governing bodies to adhere to any national pay scale and meet the needs of individual schools. Without a national pay scale there can be no coherent career structure for teachers. For example, because of financial constraints more and more primary schools are removing the position of deputy headteacher from their staffing establishment and secondary schools are inevitably reducing the number of deputy headteacher posts. Governing bodies are also choosing to reduce the numbers of promoted posts. Career development pathways are being eroded.

A national pay structure should be based on a basic common scale giving parity between teaching and similar graduate occupations. Much consideration needs to be given to the ways in which teachers are able to progress up the salary scale. There would be considerable difficulties in using appraisal or performance-related pay in the development of a coherent career structure. There should not be different basic scales for teachers of different subjects. Particular consideration needs to be given to ensuring comparability for teachers in mid-career.

Teaching should, of course, remain an all-graduate profession. New teachers should start on a common entry point with additional points for experience. The situation presents difficulties for mature, newly qualified teachers who are more expensive to employ than their younger colleagues. The importance of considering the effects of the current imbalanced gender profile alongside the failure to retain young teachers cannot be overestimated, particularly within the context of the number of teachers seeking early retirement. Conditions of service should provide for relevant induction for new teachers and for returners.

Careful consideration needs to be given to the entry point for returners, which ideally should be based on their previous salary and experience. Similarly, supply teachers' salaries should be based on their previous salary and experience with added experience as a supply teacher accumulated for progression up the salary scale. It is a disgrace that there is evidence to show that current financial constraints make experienced teachers too expensive to employ. Experience outside teaching should be acknowledged according to criteria relevant to education. National pay structures must apply to all teachers as well as centrally managed services. There should be no differentiated pay rates for different schools. Flexibilities, which give governors substantial powers to determine salaries, should be considerably reduced. Steps should be taken to ensure that the need for a fair and equitable pay scale is acknowledged. The current concept of promotion, furthermore, moves teachers away from pupils. Teachers should automatically qualify for additional points for experience in teaching and for achieving recognized additional and further qualifications while in service, regardless of their point on the salary scale. This would, of course, have financial implications and would have to be addressed within the concept of formula funding. There may be some benefits in giving consideration to a process of re-accreditation, for example by adopting a scheme similar to that which teacher colleagues in the USA report is being introduced in Massachusetts.

Career development should be apparent through the use of promoted posts for additional responsibilities. Each responsibility should attract an additional point awarded by the governing or relevant body, following application and interview in an open and competitive process. Deputy headteacher posts should be mandatory for all schools, including two-teacher schools, and their pay should be subject to a separate scale along with the headteachers' pay scale. Governing bodies should retain responsibility for compiling an appropriate pay policy document for the school detailing, among other things, the staffing structure, the nature of promoted posts and procedures for advertising and appointment.

Involvement, beyond the traditional pattern of teaching practice, with Initial Teacher Education should be recognized within the scope of additional responsibility points and not be left to the discretion of governing bodies. There is little doubt that such involvement is seen as a positive contribution towards professional and career development. This role should be acknowledged and rewarded with all higher education institutions paying schools appropriately for involvement in ITE.

National pay structures, alongside conditions of service, need to consider controls over the use of temporary contracts. These should only be issued for certain specific reasons such as maternity leave, long-term sickness, filling vacancies prior to permanent appointments being made and other identified short-term needs. Part-time teachers should not be appointed automatically onto temporary contracts nor should temporary contracts be used as a quality control mechanism for newly qualified teachers who need guaranteed appropriate conditions of service and the entitlement to an induction period. There is a lot to be said for the concept of a properly funded and organized probationary period.

The current salary structure was determined to meet the needs of secondary schools. Serious consideration needs to be given to providing parity of opportunity for teachers in primary schools with colleagues in secondary, and special, education. Teachers in centrally managed services should also have parity with their colleagues in schools. There should be no need for additional posts for recruitment and retention nor for excellence points nor any form of performance-related pay.

A common pay scale for heads and deputies should provide for an element of incremental progression rather than the current system of spot payments and additional payments at the discretion of governing bodies. Careful attention, however, needs to be given to differentials. Although it is acknowledged that some consideration has to be acknowledged in relation to the size of the school, the current system rewards the heads of small schools unfairly. When considering the levels of responsibility held it cannot be considered fair and reasonable for some primary headteachers to be paid less than many secondary teachers. In large schools, the headteacher has a number of people to whom tasks can be delegated. In small schools the headteacher has to carry a disproportionate level of administrative responsibility, very often in addition to having full teaching responsibilities. If appropriate national pay scales were developed, then individual governing bodies would not need to award additional discretionary payments.

NATIONAL CONDITIONS OF SERVICE

The 1987 Teachers Pay and Conditions Act, amended in 1991, established national conditions alongside pay. However, none of the succeeding annual documents has addressed the issues raised. Although the concept of directed time was established, setting down for the first time teachers' contractual hours, other workload related issues have only been given lip-service by the Review Body and IAC.

Proper funding of the education service and resourcing of schools would enable schools to employ appropriate non-teaching staff to support the provision of effective teaching and learning. This would release teachers from many of the non-teaching duties they currently have to undertake. If nothing else, if all schools were able to employ a full-time school clerk, a full-time caretaker or site supervisor and a full-time nursery nurse in primary schools, this would have a significant impact upon the workload of teachers and the quality of teaching and learning.

Teachers' working time needs to be defined more appropriately and workload issues need to be addressed. The introduction of directed time was considered initially to be an insult to professionalism. The expectation that additional work should be undertaken outside this specified time has contributed to workload pressures. Consideration has to be given to the provision of time away from direct pupil contact in addition to 'Monitoring and Support Time (MAST)' (Select Committee, 1994, para. 64). This could usefully be described as 'Desk Time' following the example of Norwegian teachers' conditions of service. This 'Desk Time', including MAST, for all teachers regardless of their level of responsibility should be 20 per cent of the time that children are in school and would enable teachers to undertake duties which are in addition to their direct teaching responsibilities. All teachers, including heads and deputies, should have specified teaching duties. Headteachers of small schools should not, however, be expected to undertake full-time class-teaching responsibilities.

There should be minimum staffing levels for all schools with mandatory maximum class sizes, although there needs to be some flexibility to allow individual schools to organize appropriately according to their situations. In the current Teachers' Pay and Conditions Document there is a limit to the amount of supply cover teachers are expected to undertake. In practice this is often difficult to achieve. There needs to be a clear contractual limit to the amount of cover individual teachers actually undertake.

Conditions of service must address the question of induction for new teachers and support for returners. However, before a coherent induction strategy can be developed, consideration needs to be given as to when Qualified Teacher Status (QTS) is awarded. The probationary year has been removed and new teachers are frequently appointed to schools on temporary contracts. Despite the new requirements of the Teachers Pay' and Conditions Order for headteachers to consider induction needs, there is no mechanism to enable this to happen in a consistent manner. If a period of properly funded induction were linked with the award of QTS this would have considerable benefits for individual teachers and the quality of teaching and learning provided within a school.

The question of statutory entitlement to in-service education and training (INSET) has to be addressed. The inclusion of continuous professional development within the remit of the Teacher Training Agency may be a step towards this objective. The current arrangements revolving around the five pupil-free days are far from satisfactory. Teachers should be entitled to release with pay in order to undertake INSET. There should be a scale for release giving the opportunity of, for example, one term for each five years of service. Teachers should also be entitled to apply for grant support to attend higher education and other award bearing courses. Conditions of service have to include the development of properly funded and organized systems of appraisal. Appraisal for professional development purposes should be an entitlement for all teachers. In a period of contraction teachers should also have opportunities to undertake job exchanges, and inducements to encourage governing bodies to facilitate such developments should be considered.

CONCLUSIONS

This chapter has given an indication of how a number of issues, identified over the recent past as crucial to the recruitment and retention of a high quality teaching force, need to be reconsidered within the framework of the development of an alternative funding formula for education as a whole. There is no doubt that the vast majority of teachers remain totally committed to the children and young people they teach. At the same time, no external observer can dispute the stresses being caused as a result of a lengthy period of imposed change coupled with inequities in current pay and conditions, exacerbated by financial constraints.

Teachers may show commitment but the numbers leaving because of ill health and stress-related problems is a national scandal. It is also a scandal that in general teachers do not command equivalent salaries to those of other graduates and are expected to work in conditions which often infringe basic health and safety requirements. A proper career structure with appropriate conditions of service must offer rewards which are equitable and fair and which offer comparability within education and across the professions generally.

These views are written with an eye on the ideal world but nothing is ever achieved if nothing is ever expected. On behalf of teachers currently in service and those yet to come, and of the children currently within the statutory education service and those yet to come, teachers are urged to work together, regardless of sector, teacher association or political views. Policy-makers are urged to address the issues raised as a matter of urgency.

REFERENCES

Beloff, M. (1985) 'Education – The Enemy Within.' *Daily Telegraph*, 27 Nov. 1995.

Busher, H. and Saran, R. (1992) *Teachers' Conditions of Employment: A Study in the Politics of School Management*. The Bedford Way Series, University of London Institute of Education: Kogan Page.

DES (1986) *Education (No. 2) Act*. London: HMSO.

DES (1988) *Education Reform Act*. London: HMSO.

DfE (1995) *School Teachers' Pay and Conditions Document 1995*. London : HMSO.

Elliott, J. (1992) *The Future of Initial Teacher Training* (a letter sent on behalf of the British Educational Research Association Task Group on Teacher Education to the National Commission on Education).

Healy, G. and Kraithman, D. (1994) *Evidence to The School Teachers' Review Body*. University of Hertfordshire.

Hewton, E. (1986) *Education in Recession: Crisis in County Hall and Classroom*. London : Allen and Unwin.

House of Commons (1994) *The Disparity in Funding between Primary and Secondary Schools*. Education Committee Second Report, Vol. 1; Report together with the proceedings of the committee. London: HMSO.

Interim Advisory Committee on School Teachers' Pay and Conditions (1988–91) *First to the Fourth Reports*. London: HMSO.

Lawrence, I. (1992) *Power and Politics at the Department of Education and Science*. London: Cassell.

National Commission on Education (1993) *Learning to Succeed: A Radical Look at Education Today and a Strategy for the Future*. London: Heinemann.

National Union of Teachers (1986–95) *Annual Reports*. NUT.

National Union of Teachers (1994) *Recruit Retain Motivate: Fourth Submission to the School Teachers' Review Body*. NUT.

Office of Manpower Economics (1995) *Consultative Document on Possible Modifications to the Pay Structure for Classroom Teachers*. Letter on behalf of School Teachers' Review Body.

School Teachers' Review Body (1992–95) *First to Fourth Reports*. London: HMSO.

Teacher Training Agency (1995) *Platform*, Spring 1995, 1. TTA and the Central Office of Information.

Vaizey, J. (1984) 'Schoolroom savings – the £7bn equation.' *Director Journal*, September 1984.

Wadsworth, A. (1995) *Review of the Promotion of Teaching as a Career*. Undertaken for the Teacher Training Agency.

Wilkin, M. (ed.) (1992) *Mentoring in Schools*. London: Kogan Page.

Wragg, T. (1995) *Teaching for the Learning Society*. Edited transcript of an address to the North of England Education Conference. *Developing the Learning Society*. North Yorkshire County Council/the University of York.

Chapter 4

The Need to Cope with Change

Horace Bennett

> Neglect of the phenomenology of change – that is, how people actually experience change as distinct from how it might have been intended – is at the heart of the spectacular lack of success of most social reform.
>
> (Fullan, 1991)

INTRODUCTION

In this chapter it will be argued that between the Scylla of seeing the management of change as the macho exercise of raw power and the Charybdis of seeing change as essentially unmanageable in an unpredictable world, it is possible to steer a difficult but navigable route by recognizing one's own difficulties when faced by the unknown and using this understanding to be sensitive to the difficulties of others in order to help them make sense of the realities they share with us.

The need to cope with change in today's schools can be seen to be necessary at various levels: the global, the institutional and the individual. This chapter will make reference to the turbulence of the general environment in which we have to function, before considering the individual's needs in coping with change and the institutional imperative to create the kind of climate in which change can genuinely flourish.

Alvin Toffler (1980) argues that we are in a period of transition which exceeds in its intensity and pace of change the transition between the agrarian and the industrial waves of social revolution. We are sandwiched between the industrial and the technological ages. Everything is called into question – our religious and social beliefs, our stabilities and certainties to the extent that:

> Nothing is more dangerous than yesterday's success ... The very habits that have helped (us) succeed have become counter-productive.

The plethora of government educational initiatives in the last decade have done little to reassure us that we will soon reach a period of stability and consolidation, despite the recent pronouncements of the latest Secretary of State for Education.

In such turbulent environments, it is important to adapt, for 'organisations that don't learn at a faster rate than the environment changes will eventually die' (Hoyle, 1973). Schön (1971) reminds us, on the other hand, that: 'organisations are dynamically conservative; that is, they fight like mad to remain the same.'

The challenge facing those people managing change in our schools is to achieve the great balancing act between change and stability. Kanter (1983) points out that there is 'no direct relationship between environmental pressure for change and changes themselves': there are key figures in all organizations who mediate between the outside world and its pressures to change overnight and the inside world of the organization which can only cope with so much change at a time. Even so, most organizations, if they are to survive, need to establish an 'organic' (Kanter) task culture which can form a team quickly to respond rapidly to a new challenge and then break up until such time as they, or a task group like them, are required again. Meanwhile, the 'mechanistic' structure continues to cope with the everyday routine processes and practices. Elliott-Kemp (1982) conceives of a similar overlay of organizational structure upon structure but for him it is tripartite: a steady state, proactive and reactive system which can enable the organization to maintain a balance between 'getting things done, or administration; doing new things, or innovation; reacting to crisis, or salvation' (Bell and Maher, 1986).

If organizations are dynamically conservative then so are the majority of individuals. Fullan (1991) refers to the 'joys of mastery' but acknowledges that they will be preceded by the 'anxieties of uncertainty'. The Japanese have a phrase for this ambiguous attitude to change – 'dangerous opportunity' – a phrase which accurately sums up the mixture of trepidation and excitement which characterizes many of us at the threshold of the unknown.

Alan Coulson (1985) reminds us that our anxieties can reach the level of fear and, although, along with Susan Jeffers (1991) we should feel the fear and do it anyway, he counsels all managers of change to expect resistance to any challenge to the *status quo*. It is perfectly natural and reasonable, he argues, given the dissatisfaction with existing practice which change implies, for people to defend themselves and the past. The task facing the manager of change is to avoid confrontation, to listen and to isolate and thereby make explicit the perception of threat. To see the dissenters as people contributing their own experience or version of the change, to use their concerns as a prompt to modify the proposals in such a way as to address these concerns and, above all, never to seek to undermine their confidence or present practice turns the management of change from a battlefield into a collaborative exercise.

Watson (1986) similarly cautions against the creation of enemies and outcasts in arguing that all major change processes create winners and losers:

> If a situation is at all complex and the range of options for action at all controversial ... there will be costs to be borne; and different decisions are likely to lead to different patterns of 'winners' and 'losers'.

I'm not sure how comforting it is to realize that managing change has never been easy:

> There is nothing more difficult to carry out nor more doubtful of success, nor more dangerous to handle, than to initiate a new order of things. For the reformer has enemies in all who profit by the old order and only lukewarm defenders in all those who would profit from the new order.
>
> (Machiavelli, 1513)

Machiavelli, who had a somewhat pragmatic approach to this sensitive issue – people should either be 'caressed' or 'annihilated' – goes on to make a crucial point about the lukewarm reaction of human beings to change:

> The lukewarmness arises partly from fear of their adversaries who have law in their favour and partly from the incredulity of mankind who do not truly believe in anything new until they have had actual experience of it.

This suggests that there are sound reasons to change the traditional order of 'Ready, aim, fire' to 'Ready, fire, aim' (Shipman, 1974), because many people who have successfully managed change will recognize the dangers of unilateral overplanning, which precludes collective adaptation and refinement by the staff involved before and after the initial experience of the new practice. Not only do involved people feel a sense of ownership of the change but, as they can rarely predict the problems of implementation, it makes sense to involve the practitioners in the identification either of adjustments required to suit the particular context within which the change is being introduced or of the nature and degree of additional support and training required once the change begins.

Teachers need to cope with change not least because of the appalling record of unsuccessful implementation of change which has been the hallmark of change managers in the past. A number of change phenomena with which we have all become familiar remind us of this fact.

Hoyle (1973) refers to 'organisational pathos' or the discrepancy between organizational intention and its actual achievements. This is the staple theme of OFSTED inspections, revealing the gap between policy and practice, between words and deeds, between rhetoric and reality. This phenomenon may have something to do with focusing on image before improving practice but it has much to do, also, with changes which have been only half implemented, perhaps because of what Fullan terms 'false clarity' (Fullan, 1991, p. 35) or partial understanding of what is expected or because the teachers themselves have not been convinced of the need for change.

> The most fundamental form of innovation is the transformation of teachers. All other forms of innovation – in materials, pupil-groupings and so forth – are often dependent for their success upon a shift in the values of teachers.
>
> (Hoyle, 1973)

Fullan (1991, p. 37) supports this emphasis on attitudes and values when he talks about change being multidimensional. He identifies three levels of change management, each of which need consideration:

1. the possible use of new or revised materials;
2. the possible use of new teaching approaches;
3. the possible alteration of beliefs.

Another phenomenon is *innovation without change* where, in its extreme form, an organization believes it has introduced a change and its members have adopted the trappings of change but actual practice remains the same (more about the autonomous professional later!). Often this phenomenon relates to the failure to address Fullan's third dimension. A school may have provided appropriate resources and training for the introduction of mixed ability teaching but if the teachers are not convinced at the level of belief in its efficacy, then change will be cosmetic.

The myth of the 'hero-innovator' (Georgiades and Phillamore, 1975) is still a danger-ous element in organizations which have not addressed the change process seriously:

> The idea that you can produce, by training, a knight in shining armour who, loins girded with new technology and beliefs, will assault his organisational fortress and institute changes both in himself and others at a stroke. The fact of the matter is that organisations such as schools will, like dragons, eat hero innovators for breakfast.

If we can get beyond the gendered images which appear to characterize much change literature, we may well agree from our own experience that sending individuals on courses to bring back the good news is much less successful a strategy than sending out a small group together or incrementally in order to create a critical mass of committed individuals and provide a support group for each other.

The successful management of change, then, at the most fundamental level, is about ensuring that teachers perceive a need for change and that they perceive that the proposed change will actually benefit themselves and the pupils in some way. It is therefore less about managing a process external to the individual and rather more about helping individuals to manage change more effectively for themselves.

Bernard Shaw warned us about reformers who 'have the idea that change can be achieved by brute sanity' and Marris (1975, quoted in Fullan, 1991) emphasizes the same need for the change manager to open the mind hermetically sealed at birth and to try to understand the change from the perspective of the practitioner:

> No one can resolve the crisis of reintegration on behalf of another. Every attempt to pre-empt conflict, argument, protest by rational planning, can only be abortive: however reasonable the proposed changes, the process of implementing them must still allow the impulse of rejection to play itself out. When those who have power to manipulate changes act as if they have only to explain, and when their explanations are not at once accepted, shrug off opposition as ignorance or prejudice, they express a profound contempt for the meaning of lives other than their own.

To manage change without the consent of the people who have to put it into practice, apart from ethical considerations, is highly problematic, especially in professional contexts. Indeed, the most successful organizations, whether inside or outside the educational field, encourage the involvement of all staff:

> Making the power available to people at all levels of organisations to take action to intro-duce or experiment with new strategies and practices, often seen as a luxury of rich times, is in fact a necessity for survival in difficult times.
>
> (Kanter, 1983)

THE AUTONOMOUS PROFESSIONAL

How, then, have traditional approaches to organizational change foundered on the rock of the autonomous professional? The anonymous, but probably typical, American teacher who admits that he knows the school's goals but carries on doing what he believes in spite of them illustrates the situation perfectly. How can we get the herd heading roughly west when there is so much capacity for individual teachers to disap-pear up a dry gulch?

Change managers need to recognize the limitations of rational planning and adopt appropriate strategies to cope with them. Most of us are familiar with the swamp (Fig.

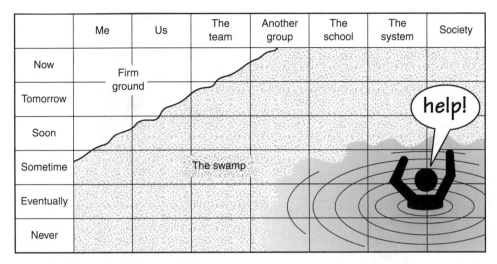

Figure 4.1 *Beware the swamp.*
Source: B. Hopson and M. Scally (1984) *Build Your Rainbow*. Likeskills Associates.

4.1): the chances of two people working together on a short-term basis are reasonably high. As soon as we become more ambitious and involve increasing numbers of others and we try to extend our collaboration over a significant time-span we create for ourselves an exponential number of opportunities for misunderstanding, circumstantial obstacles and variable practice.

To return briefly to our earlier theme of Toffler's lack of stabilities and certainties, it is interesting to compare Weick's view of the educational world in 1976 with today's reality. He created the image of the educational playing field (Fig. 4.2), an elliptically shaped pitch which is on a camber to allow the ball to run about uncontrollably. In place of the conventional fixed goal posts, you need to envisage a large number of goal posts, all of which are capable of being moved at a moment's notice. The referee or headteacher is trying to ensure the game is played according to the rules but the task is complicated by the fact that all the pupils have their own version of the rules (and are actually invited to negotiate on such matters as their progress and aims), by the contributions of the coaches or teachers, everyone of whom believes him or herself to have a clearer perception than the referee, and by the actions of spectators (parents, LEA advisers, inspectors, governors, government quangos) who might enter the field without prior notice to score a goal of their own. The relatively simple aim of heading west can be occasionally stampeded by so much conflicting and often unsolicited advice.

Cohen, March and Olsen (1972) challenge us to reconsider our assumptions that organizations take decisions in a rational way. They posit a theory relating to American universities which can perhaps be replicated in the practice of all organizations to a greater or lesser degree. A meeting is conceived of as a garbage can into which is thrown people, problems, emotions, time and energy. Attendance at meetings is variable in that you may have an influential person at an early meeting who nudges the decision in one direction, yet he or she is replaced at a subsequent meeting by a new influential player with a different perspective, and the decision shifts in the opposite direction. People arrive at meetings with emotions which have nothing to do with the meetings; for instance, they may have just fallen out with a colleague or have had an

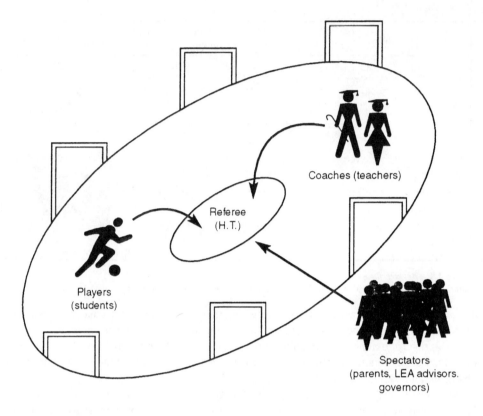

Score: Education 0
        Others 26

Figure 4.2   *Educational goals.*
Source: Weick (1976) 'Educational organisations as loosely-coupled systems.' In *Administrative Science Quarterly*, **21** (1 March)

altercation with a recalcitrant pupil: this affects their capacity for straight thinking. People arrive at meetings with hobby-horses which they take to all meetings irrespective of the agenda ('When I was at Bristol . . . ') and they also arrive with preconceived solutions to problems as yet unidentified. They bring with them variable amounts of time and energy to deal with the problems. The result of all these factors congregating at a meeting is that the decision-making process is perceived perhaps as flawed and completely arbitrary and the meeting itself is reduced to little more than meaningless ritual. A more positive perception might be to recognize that all of our lives, whether personal or organizational, are concerned with making decisions based on less than ideal levels of information and seeking to implement them with and through real people who may or may not behave predictably.

This uncomfortable assault on our assumptions is compounded by Weick (1976) who expounds the notion of loose-coupling. This asserts the fact that in all professional organizations there is only a tenuous link between organizational direction and the direction of the individuals within it:

Coupled events are responsive to some extent but there is always a strong inclination towards preservation of individuality, identity, autonomy.

This principle can be applied to all levels, so, in school terms, there is only a loosely coupled relationship between one school and other schools (though it could be tenuously argued that the National Curriculum has gone some way towards securing the link more firmly), between what the school says it is about and what is happening in the class-rooms, between means and ends and between what teachers ask of pupils and what they get in return.

Weick (1976) argues that in terms of reduced resources and accountability pressures, we cannot afford to spend significant amounts of time on goal identification and then 'the organisation proceeds as if the activity were only an exercise.'

Shipman (1974) believes that the traditional attempt to set institutional aims and then expect individuals to follow them should be reversed by a consideration of classroom realities, from which aims may ultimately be derived:

Teachers talk, then they move onto activities, they examine the whole school programme, they raise philosophical issues and then they struggle with goals.

The main implication for managers of change in schools is to rely rather less on detailed blueprints and lengthy meetings trying to achieve an unlikely consensus and rather more time on tuning into where people actually are in terms of their practice and supporting them through change. This is not to deny the value of a rational approach to the planning of change but it does indicate that this is a necessary but not sufficient condition for its effective implementation. Only the active processes of monitoring, supporting and coaching are capable of bringing about the necessary shifts in attitude which accompany the 'joys of mastery'.

INDIVIDUAL ATTITUDES TO CHANGE

Harvey Jones (1989) simultaneously alerts us to the difficulties facing the would-be teacher of adults and emphasizes the importance of a positive climate to encourage growth:

My own experience of trying to teach and train managers is that it is extremely difficult to teach grown-up people anything. It is however relatively easy to create conditions under which people teach themselves.

Kanter (1983) in Fig. 4.3 ironically recommends the creation of a climate of growth through ignoring ideas from 'below', making it difficult to gain approval to act, threat-ening dismissal for failure, regarding problem identification as a sign of the discoverer's incompetence, management secrecy and so on.

This implied sensitivity of individuals to the climate in which they work and the ways in which they are treated is reinforced by Egan (1982). Egan provides a useful psycho-logical perspective on individuals and change. He points out that it is not easy to receive help and this is particularly true in professional contexts where there is an expectation that the individual is self-sufficient. To ask for help in some climates is tantamount to admitting incompetence, weakness and an inability to cope. Small wonder if people in such an atmosphere pretend to themselves and others that they fully under-

---

1.   Regard any new idea from below with suspicion – because it's new and because it's from below.

2.   Insist that people who need your approval to act first go through several other levels of management to get their signatures.

3.   Ask departments or other individuals to challenge and criticize each other's proposals (that saves you the job of deciding; you just pick the survivor).

4.   Express your criticisms freely, and withhold your praise. (That keeps people on their toes.) Let them know that they can be fired anytime.

5.   Treat identification of problems as signs of failure, to discourage people from letting you know when something in their area isn't working.

6.   Control everything carefully. Make sure people count anything that can be counted, frequently.

7.   Make decisions to reorganize or change policies in secret and spring them on people unexpectedly. (That also keeps them on their toes.)

8.   Make sure that requests for information are fully justified, and make sure that it is not given out to managers freely. (You don't want data to fall into the wrong hands.)

9.   Assign to lower-level managers, in the name of delegation and participation, responsibility for figuring out how to cut back, lay off, move people around or otherwise implement threatening decisions you have made and get them to do it quickly.

10.   And, above all, never forget that you, the higher ups, already know everything important about this business.

'By enouraging innovation and entrepreneurship at all levels, by building an environment in which more people feel included, involved and empowered to take initiative, companies as well as individuals can be the masters of change.'

Figure 4.3   *Ten rules for stifling innovation.*
Source: R. M. Kanter (1983) *The Changemasters*. London: Allen and Unwin.

stand what they are being asked to do and end up producing something a long way away from the change manager's expectations. It is difficult, Egan says further, to commit oneself to change. This reminds us of individual reluctance to take on a new practice which may reveal a lack of skill on our part. Klein (1965) helps us to understand why we justify the *status quo* in such situations when proposed changes threaten us. We tend to rationalize our behaviour by projecting alternative behaviours onto others: 'Thus we can avoid looking at our own fear of change and deny our secret wish to keep things comfortably as they are.'

Teachers who play safe in the classroom by setting tasks for pupils which are easy to manage but may not challenge or demand initiative on the part of the learner may easily justify such a course by projecting the inner desire to create a more exciting learning environment onto college and university lecturers: 'It's OK for them to be idealistic, they haven't to face 35 children on a daily basis.' Similarly, they project their guilt feelings onto ultra-conservative figures who may stereotypically take the form of parents or certain education ministers: 'I'm putting the pupils through this back-to-basics activity because the parents don't want trendy techniques and neither does the government.' In this way, the teacher justifies the *status quo* and refuses to engage in what might potentially be a painful process initially in terms of learning and adopting new practices. Klein is clear about the need to avoid creating scapegoats and dividing staff into participators and non-participators; it is far more constructive to explore the reasons why people are reluctant to engage (and it is likely to prove to be different reasons for a range of people) and to find ways of reducing the threat and easing them into a situation where they will not have to lose face. Often, once people have been persuaded to become involved, the eventual feelings are positive ones but they need to be supported as they make the leap of faith into unknown territory: 'change efforts have to mobilise people around what is not yet known ... They require a leap of imagination' (Kanter, 1983).

Klein suggests that the leap is rarely easy:

> This means we have to take back into ourselves either the enthusiasm or the boredom, the eagerness or the reluctance which we have projected onto others ... It results in a resumption of the inner conflict and is therefore sometimes painful.

The change manager's role is similarly problematic:

> the essence of the task of constructive leadership is to foster a climate of security and openness which enables identity and corporate commitment to flourish without the need for scapegoats and adversaries.
>
> (Klein, 1965)

Presumably, educational reformers at government levels would argue that an external compulsion to change (usually legislative, occasionally resource-driven) is necessary to force people into a new situation within which they will eventually experience an attitude shift. Those engaged in researching changes in schools might, on the other hand, question the extent to which *real* change has been brought about in the classroom rather than at the level of policy and rhetoric.

Egan reminds us, too, that 'it is difficult to submit to the influence of a helper; help is a threat to esteem, integrity and independence.' This emphasizes the need for sensitivity when offering support; the *kind* of support and the relationship between the persons providing and receiving help are critical factors in determining how much learning will take place. Not only should the relationship allow for the admission of difficulty in understanding but the person providing that help needs to adopt an appropriate style of support on a continuum from direction to delegation, depending upon the experience and skills of the person receiving the help. An inexperienced teacher new to the organization may welcome advice and even prescription if this shortens the learning process and saves the need to reinvent the wheel. However, experienced teachers would probably want a much less obvious degree of support, perhaps a modicum of coaching with an opportunity to shape the change themselves.

Finally, Egan tells us 'it is not easy to see one's problems clearly at first', which indicates that in the early stages of changes we are being asked to change in so many ways simultaneously that we are unsure of the exact nature of the help we require. This factor further emphasizes the importance of getting to grips with the tasks before final adjustments and refinements are made. It is not until we actually experience the changes in practice that we fully appreciate the extent of the change we are implementing. Providing support too early may, therefore, be counter-productive.

The classic bereavement or transition curve (Adams *et al.*, 1976) (Fig. 4.4), normally applied to traumatic changes in our personal lives, is equally applicable in any period of significant professional change. The initial reaction of shock which renders us incapable of action is often replaced by a phase of minimization in which we deny the significance

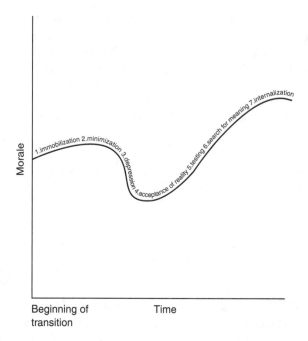

Figure 4.4   *The transition curve.*
Source: J. D. Adams *et al.* (1976) *Transition: Understanding and Managing Personal Change.* London: Robertson

and scale of the demands upon us; it can be hours, days or weeks later before the full enormity of what we are facing finally sinks in. Gradually, we begin to accommodate ourselves to the change, to accept its inevitability and to begin to test out the details as we engage. Eventually, in successful change processes, we make sense of the change for ourselves and begin to link our old skills with the new demands of the situation until we finally wonder what all the fuss was about. The easiest way to illustrate this process for ourselves is to think of a real example, such as an OFSTED inspection, and to think back to our feelings at the various stages.

Different changes impact upon different individuals in different ways, so the successful manager of change is aware that some staff are at the end of the continuum which might be described as 'active support', demonstrating co-operation and commitment, while others are at the opposite extreme of 'active resistance' which manifests itself in subversion and sabotage. In between the extremes lie the indifferent and the apathetic.

Finally, Fig. 4.5 demonstrates how the readiness (i.e. willingness to listen and to be involved in change) of an individual depends upon a number of factors and those same factors produce an organizational climate of readiness to change.

Mechanic (1967, quoted in Dunham 1984) emphasizes the significance of coping skills in determining the perceived degree of threat:

> If we are to understand the stress situation of a man falling out of a boat, the main determinant of how much stress he experiences will be whether or not he can swim.

and precisely the same principles apply here. Where an individual feels she/he has the skills and knowledge to transfer to the new situation, where their self-esteem, capacity to tolerate ambiguity and sense of motivation are reasonably high, they will be in a state

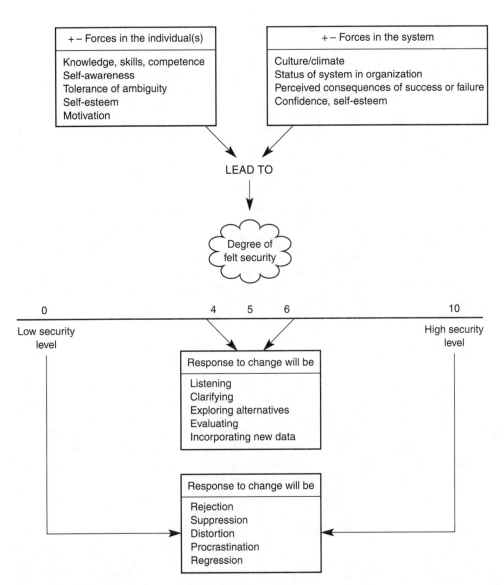

Figure 4.5 *Diagnosing readiness to change.*

of readiness to assimilate new ideas and practices. Teams, departments, faculties which have an open and trusting climate, are well-regarded within the school as a whole, know they will be rewarded, even in failure, and which have a good track record in successful innovation will exhibit similar characteristics of readiness.

What is interesting is that where individuals or groups have either very positive or very negative forces at work, the readiness to change will be low. We have probably all experienced individuals and situations where morale is so low that change is unthinkable and, conversely, where there has been such complacency and 'touch-me-not-ness' evident that change is equally inconceivable. The optimum environment for change to flourish lies somewhere between these two extremes.

Teachers on courses find it illuminating to consider colleagues involved in change as individuals rather than as members of groups and find it useful to consider their readiness as well as their capability to change (Everard and Morris, 1990). Blanket 'solutions' or approaches rarely meet individual needs and can be counter-productive. It is quite likely that some individuals will have all the necessary skills to effect change but a negative attitude; in such cases, all the training in the world will not bring about the shift required – it is essential to explore the attitudinal difficulty. Conversely, a highly motivated and enthusiastic newcomer may demonstrate a perfect readiness for change but be completely lacking in the pertinent skills. An analysis of this kind, particularly where the individuals concerned are involved in the process, is much more likely to lead to a successfully differentiated support programme for effective implementation of change than any broad sweep strategy. Once again, however, it would be arrogant to make assumptions on behalf of others without involving them in the analysis of need.

This section has emphasized the importance of considering the implementers of change as individuals rather than categorizing them crudely as 'innovators' or 'laggards', 'rational adopters' or 'stone-age obstructionists' (Dalin *et al.*, 1977–8). The most reluctant of participators may, deep down, be capable of responding to a sensitive approach even if, ultimately, self-interest is the fundamental pressure for change.

A VIEW FROM THE BRIDGE

The management of change is at most times an unpredictable and messy business and the reality of successful change may be that its orchestration in terms of step-by-step implementation is actually a superimposed figment of someone's imagination. Like a well-told tale, it is likely in its construction to gain from convenient amnesia and creative elaboration. The true realities of a change process are only to be determined by a collation of the unilateral perspectives of all the individuals involved. Often, the 'strategic direction' may have been an afterthought rather than a precursor of the experience.

Having said this, it is useful to the manager of change to employ a variety of means to gain an overview of the change as it happens. It is important to be aware, for instance, that we are not dealing with a set of static challenges: the major elements of the change process – the nature of the change itself, the social and working context in which it takes place and the role and perspective of the change manager over time – are all interrelated, mutually influential and constantly shifting. For example, in introducing a positive behaviour policy into a school, the 'model' selected is likely to be refined and adapted to suit the culture of the school; the ways that staff relate to pupils and to other members of staff both formally and socially may be significantly altered over time and the member of staff introducing the change may have to adopt a range of roles in order to facilitate its introduction, development and implementation.

Leavitt's diamond (1965) illustrates this interdependence of the structures, tasks, people and systems in an organization. When a new organizational structure such as a faculty or curriculum team is created, it inevitably affects the ways staff relate to each other in the formal sense and will inevitably bring about shifts in roles and the kinds of tasks to be completed. Similarly, bringing in a new member of staff will affect existing patterns of relationships and may, depending upon how influential he/she is, affect the way staff are grouped and the kinds of jobs they perform. A skilful manager of change will weigh up the particular situation and decide whether to start by introducing new people and investing in the training of existing staff or whether to bring about new groupings of staff which will act as a catalyst for shifting the emphasis of the priorities and tasks to be delivered. Recent thinking (Fullan, 1993) suggests that research would indicate that successful management of change is rarely achieved by structural changes in advance of a shift in perception.

In this regard, Lewin's concept (1951) of unfreezing, changing and refreezing may be unhelpful in a period of rapid change in that, having seen how difficult it is to move people away from established practices, it makes little sense to embed new practices so firmly that future adaptation will be problematic. At the same time, while wishing to create a culture with a constant capacity to adapt and modify, it is worth reminding ourselves about the human need to experience some stability. Fullan's concept of 'institutionalization' (1991, p. 49) introduces a slightly different angle on this issue by implying that practices which do not become embedded in organizational operations are subject to 'blunting' and reversion to old practices. Ultimately, a balance needs to be struck between creating sufficient stability for human comfort, supporting innovation to ensure a reasonably consistent outcome and avoiding the suggestion that the new practice represents the final solution.

Force-field analysis has been a recognized tool for allowing change managers to look systematically and holisticly at a situation, although a less sophisticated Strengths, Weaknesses, Opportunities and Threats analysis (SWOT) or even a pros and cons approach can serve the purpose. It envisages the *status quo* in a given situation as a vertical line which is held in position by equally balanced forces exerting themselves in opposite directions. The line can be moved in the desired direction by either increasing the driving forces or decreasing the restraining forces. The degree of sophistication in the model can be increased by dividing the challenge being faced into various levels or categories: factors external to the school, whole school issues, departmental or team, individual, personal and so on. It may be further refined by drawing horizontal lines of varying lengths to indicate forces of different strength or power (Fig. 4.6). This enables the planner to see at a glance the strengths and positive forces which will help to drive the initiative forward and the weaknesses or actively negative forces which will inhibit and counteract its achievement. From here, it is possible to devise ways of reinforcing and developing the drivers as well as ways of reducing the restrainers, thereby tackling the change from both directions. Used intelligently, with due recognition of its imprecision (based as it is on perception), it may provide a useful overview.

Kotter and Schlesinger's categories (1979) offer us a different kind of overview in suggesting that successful change management involves selecting from a range of change strategies, some of which carry quite strong moral overtones, and being prepared to employ a variety of strategies at different strategic points in the change process (see Table 4.1). Many changes facing schools today, for example, have been initiated through legislative pressure with a powerful coercive element. Once the inertia inhibiting change has been overcome in this way, however, successful change managers are able to use educative, participative and facilitative strategies in order to customize the initiative and involve teachers in its development and refinement. Managers who choose to use manipulative and power-coercive strategies at the school level need to be sure of their power base, at ease with their conscience and aware of the potential resentment and subversive energy they are engendering in others for the future. Managers

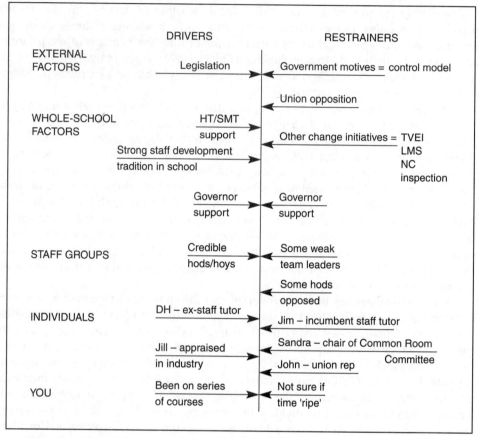

Figure 4.6 *Force-field analysis: introduction of appraisal.*

who use bargaining strategies, similarly, need to beware of creating a culture where the concessions made have to be increasingly attractive and where, eventually, no one attempts anything without first being given a sweetener of some kind!

Kanter (1983) raises some interesting issues relating to the fine line between skilful image-making which may enhance the change process and manipulation (see Fig. 4.7). 'Revision of the past' has a chillingly Orwellian ring to an activity which might, on the other hand be construed as perfectly ordinary in suggesting that as individuals we constantly influence each other's perceptions and actions. Ultimately, the decision as to whether these activities are manipulative or constructive will be based on motive. Where the change manager is seeking to save the faces of the losers, create a powerful mythology which will give people some kind of guidance to their actions and make them feel comfortable and secure with the decisions that have been perhaps irrevocably taken, it could be argued that they are following that most human of tendencies to find justification in the *status quo* as it now exhibits itself. However, we move dangerously close to playing God when our arrogance of certainty is such that we reconstruct reality on the behalf of others. (The less sensitive amongst us might wonder why there is so much fuss about an activity which is the core function of politicians, lawyers, estate agents, teachers and many other professions!)

Table 4.1 *Methods for dealing with resistance to change*

Approach	Commonly used in situations	Advantages	Drawbacks
Education + communication	Where there is a lack of information or inaccurate information and analysis.	Once persuaded, people will often help with the implementation of the change.	Can be very time-consuming if lots of people are involved.
Participation + involvement	Where the initiators do not have all the information they need to design the change, and where others have considerable power to resist.	People who participate will be committed to implementing change, and any relevant information they have will be integrated into the change plan.	Can be very time-consuming if participators design an inappropriate change.
Facilitation + support	Where people are resisting because of adjustment problems.	No other approach works as well with adjustment problems.	Can be time-consuming, expensive, and still fail.
Negotiation + agreement	Where someone or some group will clearly lose out in a change, and where that group has considerable power to resist.	Sometimes it is a relatively easy way to avoid major resistance.	Can be too expensive in many cases if it alerts others to negotiate for compliance.
Manipulation + co-optation	Where other tactics will not work, or are too expensive.	It can be a relatively quick and inexpensive solution to resistance problems.	Can lead to future problems if people feel manipulated.
Explicit + implicit coercion	Where speed is essential, and the change initiators possess considerable power.	It is speedy, and can overcome any kind of resistance.	Can be risky if it leaves people mad at the initiators.

Source: J. Kotter and L. Schlesinger (1979) 'Choosing strategies for change'. *Harvard Business Review*, **57** (2).

Those who master change know that they can never tell the truth but they also know what the truth is …

'Organizational change consists in part of a series of emerging constructions of reality, including revision of the past, to correspond to the requisites of new piayers and new demands.'

* *Individuals disappear into collectives*

Change Agents sow seeds and vanish to consolidate a sense of ownership in others.

* *Early events and people disappear and later events and people come forward*

* *Conflicts disappear into consensus*

Saving the face of those, who opposed becomes important for co-operation

* *Equally plausible alternatives disappear into obvious choices*

Champions of the idea must sell it with conviction to provide security

* *Accidents, uncertainties and muddle-headed confusions disappear into clear-sighted strategies*

Reconstructed logic. Even though strategies may only be formulated towards the end of an innovation, they are an important reassurance to users.

* *Multiple events disappear into single thematic events*

Useful in building up an image, creating an organizational saga. Successful moments are remembered, set-backs suffer from convenient amnesia.

Figure 4.7   *Change process distortions: truth and the 'truth'.*
Source: R. M. Kanter (1983) *The Changemasters*. London: Allen and Unwin

Huberman and Miles (1984) refer to a very different set of dilemmas facing change managers:

'Fidelity versus Adaptation' highlights the paradox of the change manager's desire to remain faithful to the original form of the change being introduced and the realisation that transplanted changes have to undergo acclimatisation and adaptation if they are to survive in a new climate.

'Centralised versus Dispersed Influence' raises the issue of power: management pressure to change can lead to resistance where there is no subsequent support for implementation and, conversely, teacher commitment can be developed during supported implementation. The key dilemma is to what extent the control comes from the centre or from the people implementing the change.

'Co-ordination versus Flexibility' emphasises a closely related dilemma. Should a change be orchestrated in a tight, structured manner or should the implementer be given the latitude over the means of achieving the end result? In professional contexts it would appear to be necessary to avoid close supervision.

'Ambitiousness versus Practicality' introduces the dilemma of scale: should schools attempt large, ambitious changes on the basis of the more you attempt the more you achieve or does it make more sense to pre-empt potential failure by introducing incremental change?

Saleability of change may be enhanced by making it:

* Trialable (pilot scheme)

* Reversible (can be jettisoned)

* Divisible (can be performed in stages)

* Have sunk costs (within existing resources)

* Discrete (self-contained)

* Congruent (compatible with general direction of the organization)

* Have publicity value (if successful)

Figure 4.8 *Tailor your innovation.*
Source: Kanter (1983) *The Changemasters*. London: Allen and Unwin

Elliott-Kemp (1982) would undoubtedly advocate the latter. He describes his 'Trojan Mouse' approach to change management as an 'entering wedge' strategy. Cynicism about an innovation because of its jargon or lack of feasibility can be pre-empted by encouraging its development in miniature. The careful management of a small-scale pilot with enthusiastic volunteers and generous resources should guarantee a successful platform from which to launch a more ambitious second phase.

Kanter (1983) offers similar guidelines to increase the chances of success when managing change (see Fig. 4.8).

Finally, Huberman discusses 'Career Development versus Local Capacity', arguing that successful managers of change are likely to be promoted and successful teams can become the victims of their own success. I would argue that it is a price worth paying.

Having an overview, then, is important to retain an overall sense of where an initiative is, what strategies have been and will be employed and the costs of such strategies, but it is vital to temper the purity of the vision with a recognition that too strict an adherence to it will not only be impossible but undesirably inflexible.

Chaos theory (Stacey, 1992) is a recent branch of management thinking which calls into question many of the traditional management activities of forecasting and planning, visioning and management by objectives which are deemed to be inadequate tools in a largely unpredictable world. It is argued that individuals in organizations should be shaping the future rather than trying to predict it. The successful management of change is as much about awareness of the capacity for visions and plans to go awry, given the human element as its least predictable component, as it is about knowing clearly where you want to be at some future point. That awareness and some knowledge of ways in which to offset the capacity for deflection from purpose by concentrating more on supporting and developing the realities of what is happening in classrooms rather than on policy-making and consensus-seeking is implicit in the view from the bridge: 'We were given two eyes, two ears and one mouth. Used in these proportions they are the change agent's best tools' (Plant, 1987).

Observation and careful listening enable the change agent to nudge situations forward far more effectively than glib persuasion.

Fullan (1982) is convinced that the way to manage change successfully in educational institutions is through training or 'coaching' in short bursts 'alternating between practice and training' 'over a period of several months' beginning with an assessment of where teachers 'are', a linking of present experience and practice with new theories, a period of guided practice with support and feedback and a final assessment of progress made:

> The evidence continues to accumulate that a new task-focused, continuous professional development, combining a variety of learning formats, and a variety of trainers and other support personnel, is evolving and is effective in bringing about change in practice.

In the next section, a consideration of the roles and functions of the change agent explores further strategies for dealing with the here and now.

CHANGE AGENT OPERATION

Kanter's definition of change agents (1983) carefully avoids the implication that change is always imposed from outside or above: 'Those organisations and people adept at the art of anticipating the need for, and of leading, productive change.' She elaborates at length, raising some important issues:

> Change agents are – literally – the right people in the right place at the right time ... The right people are the ones with ideas that move beyond the organisation's established practice, ideas they can form into visions. The right places are integrative environments that support innovation, encourage the building of coalitions and teams to support and implement visions. The right times are those moments in the flow of organisational history when it is possible to re-construct reality on the basis of accumulated innovations to shape a more productive and successful future.

The right people may well, then, be those operating at any level in an organization; the right places in which innovation flourishes are organizations with flexible structures and favourable attitudes which allow communication to flow freely in all directions; the right times are those opportunities taken to build on incremental changes which are beginning to shape proactively new actions and activities which move the organization forward.

Havelock (1973) identifies four roles which may be adopted by a change agent: catalyst, solution giver, process helper, resource linker (see Fig. 4.9). These roles are not mutually exclusive: indeed, it is possible to conceive of situations in which all four might be adopted at different stages of the change introduction. Within the 'client system' or, in this case, the school, the requisite sense of dissatisfaction with existing practices which initiates a perceived need for change may be created by the change agent acting as 'catalyst'. The role of 'solution giver' is a deceptively simple role. Bringing some kind of wholesale 'answer' to a school problem is unlikely given what we have said about solutions from other schools needing to be customized, but it may well be that knowledge of alternative ways of tackling the problem is useful in the consideration of a range of possible solutions. As 'process helper', the change agent may assist the change process at any number of points, creating disturbance which leads to a need for action, contributing to the decision-making process, helping with the search for possible answers, supporting the implementation, providing resources or monitoring and reviewing progress. Acting as 'resource linker', the change agent may

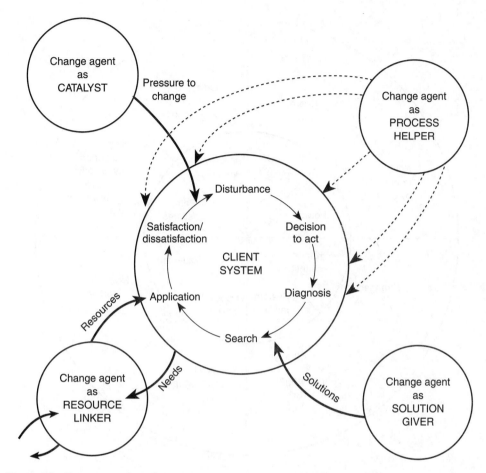

Figure 4.9 *Four ways to be a change agent.*
Source: R. G. Havelock (1973) *The Change Agent's Guide to Innovation in Education*. Educational Technical Publication

provide resources directly or orchestrate the marshalling of resources both within and from outside the school.

As the last sentence implies, a change agent may be someone from outside the school in the shape of adviser or consultant or other 'expert'. By skilfully deploying the inside and outside change agents, it is possible to avoid the disadvantages and fully exploit the advantages of each. Figure 4.10 juxtaposes the capacities of internal and external change agents.

The involved view of the internal agent may be an advantage in that they care about the school but a disadvantage in that they are too close to the problem to see it clearly, while the external agent can occasionally leave a school in a worse state than that in which it was found (!) but, as an outsider, it can see the root of the problem more easily. An external agent enjoys a brief honeymoon period (usually about ten minutes in my experience) before its expertise is challenged by the staff, whereas an internal agent finds it more difficult to escape from past failures. The external agent's lack of knowledge about the school systems and people can be compensated for by the knowledge of the internal. The internal's lack of formal power can be supplemented by the

Figure 4.10   *Insider/outsider change agents.*
Source: R. G. Havelock (1973) *The Change Agent's Guide to Innovation in Education.* Educational Technical Publications

external's freedom to speak without fear of redress and so on.

Where change agents find themselves operating from positions where they lack formal power, it becomes increasingly important that they follow Havelock's advice: to know their organization thoroughly – its structures, goals, norms and its key people (whether or not they are in positions of formal power); to look for present and potential allies; to build up their expert power by ensuring a thorough knowledge of the innovation itself and of the process of change; to empathize with adversaries in order to understand their resistance with a view to using such information positively. Finally, through persistence, they need to seek to build the internal self-renewal capacity of staff where change is the norm and innovation is rewarded even in failure.

Murgatroyd and Gray (1984) define the characteristics of such an organization:

> The self-renewing (institution) is one that sees itself in a constant state of change and development, ever open to new challenges and opportunities:
>
> 1. It thrives on human interactions;
> 2. There is a high degree of organisational awareness and high self-awareness among individual members of the team;

3. There is a climate of interpersonal warmth, a sense of sharing a task and enjoying the process of working together;
4. Those in leadership positions pay particular attention to the needs and motivation of the team as a whole and to its individual members;
5. There is a high level of genuineness. Status differences are minimised and there is little attempt to hide behind roles;
6. There is a healthy capacity for confrontation, for facing up to difficulties, particularly interpersonal ones, and for dealing with them in an open and honest way;
7. Individual team members show a high capacity for self-disclosure. They are free and caring in their encouragement of others and open and honest about their own particular weaknesses and shortcomings;
8. Communications and relationships have a quality of intimacy about them which makes for a high sense of purpose and a spirit of endeavour.

Learning organizations are essentially concerned with the management of a continuous process of change. If we accept Swieringa and Wierdsma's (1992) definition of learning 'as the changing of behaviour' and their assumption that

> Competence is not only determined by what people know or understand but also by what they can do (skills), what they have the courage and the will to do and who they are (personality and attitude)

then we will agree with them that managing change successfully is about helping individuals and organizations to manage learning effectively. We need to find ways of converting the often unconscious learning which takes place into conscious learning which can be utilized by both the individual and the organization. Swieringa and Wierdsma take this a stage further in arguing that:

> learning potential is a concept that refers to the potential to learn but in particular to the potential for learning to learn. This is sometimes called meta-learning or self-education.

Such meta-learning will only take place where the organizational climate or ethos can set up the learning conditions implicit in Murgatroyd's characteristics listed above.

This section has emphasized the dual importance of managing change through the adoption of a number of different roles as the situation and stages of change demand and of endeavouring to cultivate a positive climate for change. The need to work towards the ideal through the exercise of the expedient is illustrated by Kanter's own practicality ethic (see Conclusion). Even so, the future is shaped by today's decisions and actions rather than by visions of what may be. This means it is vitally important to work towards a series of developing and emerging visions which illuminate rather than doggedly pursue a fixed vision which will ultimately blind us to other possibilities.

CONCLUSION

Fullan (1991) points to the importance of sensitivity to 'shared senses of meaning' (p. 32) whereby individuals in organizations make sense of their lives; when we disturb these we need to do it carefully and without arrogance and we need to be sure to help people replace them with a new shared meaning about the change being introduced.

He emphasizes, too, the importance of giving attention to the 'what' and the 'how' of change:

> It is possible to be crystal clear about what one wants and be totally inept at achieving it or

to be skilled at managing change but empty-headed about what changes are most needed.

(p. 5)

It is vital, then, that managers of change make important decisions about the appropriateness of a particular change in terms of perceived need and perceived benefit as well as being expert in the management of the change process itself.

Dalin, Doyle and Ponder (1977–8) stress, too, the essential consideration of the 'practicality ethic' where overloaded teachers coping with multiple changes are concerned:

> Congruence – how will the students/pupils react and does it fit the context or situation?
> Instrumentality – clarity about how the change will be implemented (this may only fully come with actual experience of the change).
> Cost – at the end of the day will the outcomes justify the energy and time expended?

Fullan (1993) reinforces the importance of recognizing the complexities of change management and the dangers of overreliance on the rational imposition of personal or organizational visions:

> Trying to get everyone on board in advance of action cannot work because it does not connect to the reality of dynamic complexity. Understanding this process puts the concept of ownership in perspective. Ownership cannot be achieved in *advance* of learning something new.

(p. 30)

Senge (1990) reflects this important shift in the leadership function:

> The new view of leadership in learning organisations centres on subtler and more important tasks. In a learning organisation, leaders are designers, stewards and teachers. They are responsible for building organisations where people continually expand their capabilities to understand complexity, clarify vision and improve shared mental models – that is, they are responsible for learning.

This neatly takes us back to Shipman's ideas at the beginning of the chapter, starting with the classroom and then moving to goals. Looking into the telescope simultaneously through both ends provides a picture of the complex interrelationship of bottom-up and top-down activities. Beer (1990), quoted in Fullan (1993), in researching into 26 successful companies found the principle alive and well:

> isolated pockets of change reflecting new behaviours, led to new thinking which eventually pushed structures and procedures to change. People learn new patterns of behaviour primarily through their interactions with others, not through front-end training designs.

(p. 68)

What has been argued in this chapter is that the management of change should never be underestimated in terms of its complexity. It might even be asked whether it is possible to manage change in the sense of a linear progression from where we are to where we want to be. Instead of managing 'change' as an external entity, it might be more appropriate to look for a completely different role, perhaps one which has more to do with symbiosis than confrontation, which would present change as a daily task to be met by corporate effort rather than by threats to individual integrity. Dragon-slayers are only necessary where the prevailing mythology recognizes the existence of dragons or actually creates them. In the sane pursuit of individual and organizational health and a continuous climate of improvement, it will be important that professionals value each other's strengths and recognize the need to shape collectively a future which takes account of their conflicting worlds and seeks reconciliation through shared perceptions. Understanding the here and now in the classroom is the first step in that direction.

REFERENCES

Adams, J. D., Hayes, J. and Hopson, B. (1976) *Transition: Understanding and Managing Personal Change*. London: Robertson.

Beer, M., Eisenstat, R. and Spector, B. (1990) *The Critical Path to Corporate Renewal*. Boston, MA: Harvard Business School Press.

Bell, L. and Maher, P. (1986) *Leading a Pastoral Team: Approaches to Pastoral Middle Management*. Oxford: Basil Blackwell.

Cohen, M. D., March, J. G. and Olsen, J. P. (1972) 'A garbage-can model of organisational choice.' In *Administrative Science Quarterly*, **17** (2).

Coulson, A. (1985) 'The fear of change.' Unpublished paper.

Dalin, P., Doyle, W. and Ponder, G. (1977–78) 'The practicality ethic in teacher decision-making.' *Interchange*, **8** (3), 1–12.

Dunham, J. (1984) *Stress in Teaching*. London: Croom Helm.

Egan, G. (1982) *The Skilled Helper: Methods for Effective Helping*. Monterey, Calif: Brookes/Cole Pub. Co.

Elliott-Kemp, J. (1982) *Managing Organisational Change: A Practitioner's Guide*. Sheffield: PAVIC Publications.

Everard, B. and Morris, G. (1990) *Effective School Management*. London: Paul Chapman.

Fullan, M. (1982) *The Meaning of Educational Change*. Toronto: Ontario Institute for Studies in Education.

Fullan, M. (1991) *The New Meaning of Educational Change*. London: Cassell.

Fullan, M. (1993) *Change Forces – Probing the Depths of Educational Reform*. London: Falmer.

Georgiades, N. J. and Phillamore, L. (1975) 'The Myth of the Hero-Innovator: alternative strategies for organisational change.' In C. Kiernan and F. P. Woodford (eds) *Behaviour Modification with the Severely Retarded*. Associated Science.

Harvey Jones, J. (1989) *Making Things Happen: Reflections on Leadership*. London: Fontana.

Havelock, R. G. (1973) *The Change Agent's Guide to Innovation in Education*. Englewood Cliffs, N.J.: Educational Technical Publication.

Hoyle, E. (1973) 'Strategies of curriculum change.' In *In-Service Training: Structure and Content*. London: Ward Lock Educational.

Huberman, A. M. and Miles, M. B. (1984) *Innovation Up Close*. NY: Plenum Press.

Jeffers, S. (1991) *Feel the Fear and Do It Anyway*. London: Arrow.

Kanter, R. M. (1983) *The Changemasters*. London: Allen and Unwin.

Klein, M. (1965) 'Our adult world and its roots in our infancy.' *International Journal of Psycho-analysis* Vol. 1.

Kotter, J. and Schlesinger, L. (1979) 'Choosing strategies for change.' *Harvard Business Review*, **57** (2).

Leavitt, H. J. (1965) 'Applied organisational change in industry.' In J. G. March (ed.) *Handbook of Organisation*. Chicago: Rand McNally.

Lewin, K. (1951) *Field Theory in Social Science*. New York: Harper and Row.

Machiavelli, N. (1967) *The Prince*. Harmondsworth: Penguin (Original publication 1513).

Murgatroyd, S. and Gray, H. (1984) 'Leadership and the effective school.' In P. Harling (ed.) *Directions in Educational Leadership*. Lewes: Falmer Press.

Plant, R. (1987) *Managing Change and Making It Stick*. London: Fontana.

Rudduck, J. (1991) *Innovation and Change*. Milton Keynes: OUP.

Schön, D. (1971) *Beyond the Stable State*. New York: Norton.

Senge, P. (1990) *The Fifth Discipline*. New York: Doubleday.

Shipman, D. A. (1974) 'A non-model for school change.' *Educational Forum*, **38** (4).

Stacey, R. (1992) *Managing Chaos: Dynamic Business in an Unpredictable World*. London: Kogan Page.

Stewart, V. (1983) *Change: The Challenge For Management*. London: McGraw-Hill.

Swieringa, J. and Wierdsma, A. (1992) *Becoming a Learning Organisation*. Wokingham: Addison-Wesley.

Toffler, A. (1980) *Future Shock*. London: Pan Books.

Watson, L. (1986) 'The loser and the management of change.' *School Organisation*, **6** (1).

Weick, K. E. (1976) 'Educational organisations as loosely-coupled systems.' *Administrative Science Quarterly*, **21** (1 March).

Chapter 5

Developing New Skills in Teachers

Carl Parsons

INTRODUCTION

The National Curriculum, the new inspection régime, local management, grant maintained status and the individualization of schools are a set of new factors operating in education which demand the development of new skills in teachers. These factors operate to undermine the control of the intellectual and professional management of learning and emphasize a competitive, business ethic in the 'delivery' of a largely centrally defined body of learning. A second set of factors pressing in on teachers comes from a different quarter and is inconsistent with those above. The factors relate to the broader needs of pupils which teachers need to address and the wider range of outside agents with whom teachers must communicate and collaborate. The needs concern education for citizenship, relationships and parenthood, personal, social and health education and dealing with disaffection. Teachers need to relate to a number of external agents such as parents, employers and community leaders and, in respect of 'pupils with problems' (DFE, 1994), teachers need to be part of an inter-agency approach working with Social Service Departments, Health, Police and voluntary agencies.

In this chapter I will deal with the new skills needed in this developing context under the following headings:

- teaching and learning styles;
- curriculum planning and assessment;
- management and quality assurance;
- interpersonal, communication and relationship skills.

In coping with change on the scale and at the speed required, teamwork is a high priority. No school can expect all staff to develop all the skills needed. However, within the school team, roles need to be defined and the qualities and abilities developed so that the school as a corporate unit can fulfil its role in modern United Kingdom society. This role is certainly constrained and possibly deprofessionalized (Kelly, 1995), yet creative opportunities exist. These need to be built upon to retain teaching as an intellectually coherent endeavour not utterly subservient to overweening political forces and a conservatism which Ball has termed 'cultural restorations' (1994, p. 28).

The numbers of workers we are talking about here are large – 190,000 full-time equivalent primary teachers and 170,000 full-time equivalent secondary teachers in England and Wales (CIPFA, 1993). Individually, in institutional teams and as a teaching force with a history of some considerable autonomy it is necessary that such areas of autonomy that remain are strengthened or new ones staked out.

The message of this chapter, somewhat fanciful maybe, is that skills at these three levels (individual, institution, profession), under the four headings above, need to be developed.

TEACHING AND LEARNING STYLES

The challenge

Teaching and learning styles have been the focus of extensive professional debate over a long period. Arguably this *is* an area where teachers retain control – the 'how' of teaching. The National Curriculum has little to say about teaching method; the message is that it is *content* and *attainment* that are important in the National Curriculum and all that matters about methods and styles is that they should be efficient and effective.

The debates over teaching styles in primary schools have boiled on and off since the Hadow Reports (Board of Education, 1926, 1933), through Plowden (CACE, 1967) and were later informed by Bennett (1976) and the ORACLE study (Galton *et al.*, 1980). Simplistically the contest is between a traditional instructional approach to teaching and one which sets the learner in greater control. It can be represented as a set of continua with the poles defined in contrast to each other as set out in Figure 5.1.

TRADITIONAL		PROGRESSIVE
transmission	——————————	interpretation
instruction	——————————	active learning
didactic	——————————	experiential
content-focused	——————————	process-focused
homogeneous	——————————	differentiated

Figure 5.1 *Continua in the teaching/learning styles contest.*

Advocates of the right-hand column have been chastened by the judgements of the 'Three Wise Men' report (DES, 1992) where primary schooling is concerned. We struggle to find research that shows that smaller classes are more effective (Blatchford and Mortimore, 1994) so no wonder there are similar difficulties in showing that particular *styles* promote learning better (National Commission on Education, 1993). The values drawing educators towards the progressive pole(s) are not so much those of *effectiveness* as commitments to the *sorts of people* we want to produce i.e. empowered citizens capable of making informed choices for personal and communal good.

The secondary scene has been somewhat different in that student-centred learning, flexible learning and pupils taking more responsibility for their learning have been promoted by the National Council for Education Technology (NCET), the Technical and Vocational Education Initiative (TVEI) and other national bodies. While the cry has been that giving responsibility to children has let us down in primary schools, paradoxically we are urged to strive to make it happen in secondary schools.

The response

The new skills in this area that need to be greatly extended are of two linked kinds: command of a modernized psychology of learning and a better articulated rationale for the way learning is managed. Many teachers have had a long practical experience of varieties of styles of teaching. None are in ignorance of group work, active learning and resource-based learning but offering explanations convincing to professionals and public alike has never been a strength. The fact that all schools are to a greater extent self-managing – completely so in the case of GM schools – means that there is a greater impetus to plan consciously the corporate image which will include its general approach to the management of teaching and learning.

Amongst the factors said to characterize successful schools is an 'instructional emphasis' (Mortimore *et al.*, 1988). At best this will be theory-based. The theory requires a recognition that learners are varied and will each engage with the learning in their own way, bringing to it prior understandings and effective accoutrements. In many ways all teachers are social constructivists now in a post-Piaget and post-modern vein. It is not just that we *choose* to accept that children are interpreters of what we transmit; they are creators of meaning despite the meaning we think we have embedded in an activity. We can accept as well substantiated the inevitability that learners construct and reconstruct meaning, test out understanding, discard, forget and reconstitute. The renewed interest in Vygotsky (1987) is of central importance to the development of a 'scientific', communicable pedagogy. Teachers' articulation of a hard-nosed constructivist theory of learning is a key development. As Glasersfeld states:

> How could anyone be confident that the representations called up in the mind of the listener are at all *like* the representations the speaker had in mind when he or she uttered the particular words?
>
> (Glasersfeld, 1989, p. 9)

However, rather than diminishing the value of teaching this apparent loss of instructional control reorients it. Teaching is about well-targeted interventions, about challenges, about resourcing pupils' grapplings with new skills and ideas.

As a professional activity teaching relies heavily on diagnostic assessment however formally or informally conducted. Teachers are there to 'scaffold' pupils in their learning, supporting them in learning activities they would be unable to manage alone.

The work of Macrae *et al.* (1994) suggests that developing this approach to teaching is difficult. Teachers experience a tension between 'moving the lesson on and covering the ground and exercising receptiveness and patience' (p. 7). The patient analysis and scaffolding necessarily involves differentiation and sometimes individualization. With the large classes teachers are faced with, it also necessarily involves structuring learning situations where learners can 'scaffold' for fellow pupils. Collaborative group work learning has much to commend it. The new technologies also have a role to play.

This apparently progressive line is not at odds with some formal teaching. 'Telling' has its place even if we must anticipate that this most direct style of communication is to be received only partially as transmitted. We can probably agree with the Chief HMI that 'a lack of direct teaching was a third feature of unsatisfactory lessons' (OFSTED, 1995, p. 28). Teachers can strike ahead of this rather basic, unhelpful and atheoretical carp by confidently communicating a sound pedagogy.

CURRICULUM PLANNING AND ASSESSMENT

The challenge

In many respects curriculum planning and pupil assessment have been weaker aspects of teachers' work, certainly weaker than the practical management of pupils' learning. Curriculum planning is about defining the knowledge, understanding and skills to be developed, organizing the stimulus, support and resources pupils will need and carrying out assessment to see if learning and development have taken place. Often the design of learning opportunities for pupils will have to be differentiated to take account of the different starting-points or different levels of ability in the learners. The National Curriculum has removed the intellectual burden of this from teachers and set out programmes of study, attainment targets and levels of attainment for nine core and foundation studies and religious education, and, in secondary schools a modern language. The Dearing Report's (SEAC, 1994) rationalization of the centralized curriculum has still left teachers and schools with the job of implementing the plans of others. Within that remit there is scope in terms of teaching and learning styles, as discussed above, albeit within the disconnected set of subjects – integration is not encouraged! Beyond this there is a more important role to play; the *whole* curriculum is a production for which the school can take analytical, creative and moral responsibility.

The Education Reform Act 1988 places a statutory responsibility on schools to provide a curriculum which 'promotes the spiritual, moral, cultural, mental and physical development of pupils at school and of society.' This is a huge challenge. League tables and judgements of schools are made on the basis of cognitive gains and that focuses attention back onto the obvious formal segmented curriculum. HMI recorded their vision of the whole curriculum (DES, 1989a), with some non-starters as things turned out (e.g. their peddling of the 'areas of experience' framework – 'aesthetic and creative', 'linguistic and literary', etc.), but overall coverage and links between parts were there. Thus the curriculum was to be characterized by breadth, balance, relevance, differentiation, progression and continuity (DES, 1989a, pp. 42–51).

The National Curriculum Council (NCC, 1990) on whole curriculum planning reminded schools of the need to include all those other cross-curricular elements that are not statutorily required. These include economic and industrial understanding, careers, health education, education for citizenship and environmental education. Personal and social education is given a prominent place in this relegated grouping. The Chief Executive of the School Curriculum and Assessment Authority had, rather strangely, given his backing for education for citizenship harking back to Plato and Mill and stating that 'we sometimes lose sight that it [education] is about promoting social cohesion and group identity' (Tate, 1995).

The goals of personal, social and health education are also now international and the World Health Organisation's sponsorship of the European Network for the Health Promoting School is establishing the project in the countries of Europe including those of central and eastern Europe and the newly independent states (Jensen, 1995). The broader curriculum is not a narrow nationalist concern.

The National Curriculum Council published curriculum guidance documents in a number of the cross-curricular areas but it is important to note developments in relation to such matters as drugs education. In May 1995 the government launched its White Paper 'Tackling Drugs Together' and the DFE sent out a single pack to all schools containing Circular 4/95 'Drug Prevention and Schools', a 'Digest of Drug Education Resources for Schools', and a 16-page SCAA booklet 'Drug Education: Curriculum Guidance for Schools'. The pack has in handwritten style scrawled upon it the phrase 'protecting children through education'. Sex education is required by law at Key Stages 3 and 4. These are areas of social relevance for which teachers can take a major responsibility.

Pupil disaffection (Pickles, 1992), bullying (Tattum *et al.*, 1993), truancy (O'Keeffe and Stoll, 1995) and exclusions (Lovey *et al.*, 1993) are also significant ills which teachers are having to confront. There is, therefore, a challenge to thread new materials into the formal curriculum, to achieve grander goals for the individual and society, and the need to tackle social problems.

Assessment poses further problems. The criterion-referenced, ten-level attainment target related National Curriculum was hugely documented. School Assessment Folders were produced for each of the four key stages with booklets within on each subject. There was a requirement for more teacher assessment though initially it was to be subservient to standard assessments. Records of Achievement were encouraged further down the age-range and, at Key Stage 4 the relationship between levels of attainment on the ten-level National Curriculum scale and the pre-1994 GCSE grade scale was established. The much quoted phrase from the Task Group on Assessment and Testing is worth repeating.

> Promoting children's learning is a principal aim of schools. Assessment lies at the heart of the process.
>
> (DES, 1987, para. 3)

Teachers may not have been very good at assessment. Her Majesty's Chief HMI reports a degree of satisfaction with assessment in schools but also some trenchant, though poorly quantified, criticisms:

> In the great majority of schools there was insufficient planning for day-to-day assessment ... assessment information was insufficiently used for the planning of subsequent work ... Assessment information is not used to target, confirm or adapt work for individuals or groups of pupils.
>
> (OFSTED, 1995, pp. 29–30)

However, after five years (for some) pressed into service to record and report pupil attainment in National Curriculum terms they may be better. If assessment is at the heart of the process of promoting children's learning then it is diagnostic, in establishing where pupils are and where they can move on to. Assessment must also serve the reporting function. Good assessment is time-consuming. The differentiated curriculum, often required to follow from diagnostic assessment, is more time-consuming still. However, ARR (assessment, recording and reporting) is established through OFSTED (1993) as a key responsibility of the school. Done efficiently and effectively it is an integral part of a constructivist theory of learning.

The response

The technocrats have captured the central ground in curriculum making but the school can do imaginative, worthwhile work on the curriculum, establishing linkages across subjects, having cross-curricular events, exploring ways of establishing and meeting pupil needs with Dearing's released 20 per cent of the timetable.

The cross-curricular themes and dimensions can be elaborated and welded into the ethos of the school. The school can be 'the place to be' and not just a cognitive development and mechanistic learning factory. This is where we move to notions of the *good* school and not just the *effective* school (Silver, 1994) and give Bruner's (1989) 'perfink' (perceive, feel, think) a chance.

Old styles of curriculum development will not serve us well in this area where latitude is greatest. There is a need to go beyond defining objectives in subject areas and to adjust to the more subtle approach of working with *goals*, some long term and hard to evaluate, and *process*, relating these back to teaching and learning arrangements best suited to promote development towards these goals.

Let us accept that in mathematics, history and art the objectives are defined and teachers work towards them. They may not be happy with them but that is another matter. The other curriculum, the 'hidden curriculum', which paradoxically means unseen by only a few, is that mixture of interpersonal relationships (see later in this chapter), personal and social development, self-esteem and initiative, sex education, drugs education, citizenship, caring and community.

Teachers need to approach the planning and implementation in this area with a model in mind which overarches subject specific curriculum planning (see Fig. 5.2). This echoes Lawton's thesis on curriculum as a selection from culture. As the job of *what* science, geography, etc., to teach has been done, teachers can work with what are arguably the more important goals of education – the sorts of young people we want to develop, the opportunities to mature that we want them to have and the sort of self-worth and empowerment we consider that they will need. The provisions, of course, take due note of the characteristics of the pupils and community and the needs which can be derived from these sources.

The school mission statement can be pithy and vacuous. It can also be the repository of the key reference words which are a reminder and prompt to action. It may emphasize academic excellence, caring, happiness, pupil responsibility or some curricular element, e.g. music, technology. It is a pinnacle public policy slogan that should inform the curriculum audit.

Sensitive auditing of the curriculum – and let us recognize curriculum as the total experience intentionally provided by the school – requires particular analytical and diplomatic skills. There have been many approaches to audit and review (Abbotts *et al.*, 1990; Elliott-Kemp and Williams, 1980) but a bespoke audit in the 1990s needs to ask

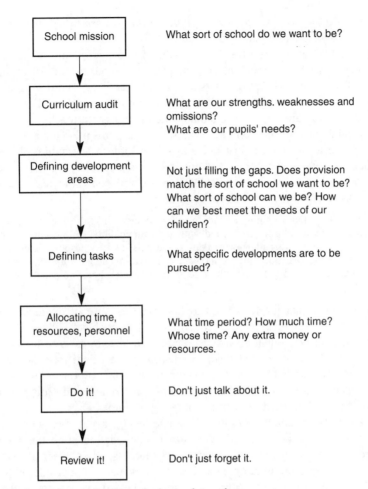

School mission	What sort of school do we want to be?
Curriculum audit	What are our strengths. weaknesses and omissions? What are our pupils' needs?
Defining development areas	Not just filling the gaps. Does provision match the sort of school we want to be? What sort of school can we be? How can we best meet the needs of our children?
Defining tasks	What specific developments are to be pursued?
Allocating time, resources, personnel	What time period? How much time? Whose time? Any extra money or resources.
Do it!	Don't just talk about it.
Review it!	Don't just forget it.

Figure 5.2   *'Whole-experience' planning and selection from culture.*

pupils, parents, governors and staff about those important personal and socially orientated goals the school should work towards. The items which present themselves for consideration are many and varied, e.g. pupil responsibility, disaffection, self-confidence, links with community and industry, drug use, staff approaches to discipline. It is a matter of what are areas of concern and what things we think we do well. Questionnaires, qualitative enquiries from within, using an external consultant, can all yield data which help to define areas for development. Somewhere in the school there need to be what amount to social research skills to conduct such an audit.

Defining development areas is never informed *only* by information. It is always, quite correctly, influenced by the values which people bring to discussions about evidence. The view *could be* that in a working-class community it is little use putting on a big anti-smoking programme or a healthy eating day. The majority view could be that discipline is OK but *still* steps should be taken to reduce the aggressive (mostly male staff) shouting at pupils to bring them to order.

Once a small number of development areas have been identified the specific tasks to be carried out to promote the development need defining. This might mean allocating a staff development day to, say, *involving pupils in the assessment of their own work* and having working teams and a follow-up enquiry.

The allocation of time, resources and personnel is a negotiating operation. Doing it and reviewing it (each development task) is plain but requires careful group organization of time if deadlines are to be met, stress avoided and successful progress made.

These are, in many respects, the skills of the action researcher (Carr and Kemmis, 1986). Certainly they are beyond the simple role of classroom teacher. Exercising these skills may capture new ground and give the school responsibility for a grander curriculum unifying role to replace the lost fields of single subject curriculum planning.

Assessment is a sharper contest. Accountability requirements are met by data served up at the end of key stages by results of standardized tasks and tests and by teacher assessment. As Brown (1990, p. 10) pointed out:

> Assessment is now (then) seen as a much broader concept and fulfilling multiple purposes. It is considered to be closely integrated with the 'curriculum' (a concept which is itself conceived in very much broader terms than in the past) and its purposes include fostering learning, improving teaching, providing valid information about what has been done or achieved, and enabling pupils and others to make sensible choices about courses, careers and other activities.

There is no doubt that teachers need to improve their use of diagnostic assessment. This would combat the criticisms made by Chris Woodhead, Chief HMI, reported earlier (OFSTED, 1995) but it is also a crucial area to gain assured public mastery. If the development of an articulated theory of learning takes hold (see the earlier section of this chapter) then its complement is diagnostic information on pupils' acquisition of knowledge, understanding and skills. And to clinch the relationship, diagnostic information needs to be *used* in the design of learning opportunities.

There needs to be an emphasis, in marking and feedback, on checks on pupils' attainment of the objectives, however this evidence is elicited; too often the assessment has been biased by considerations of quantity or neatness. It is clear that professional assessment also needs moderation and that teachers need to consult with colleagues about teaching goals, teaching techniques, approaches to assessment, what counts as successful attainment of objectives in National Curriculum terms and what counts as sufficient progress towards set goals in the broader curriculum.

In terms of the latter, applying off-the-shelf instruments which measure stress (Cook, 1992), self-esteem (Lawrence, 1988) or health behaviours (Balding, 1992) may also be an asset. Results of these need to be interpreted with due tentativeness. Added to this, for those broader curriculum goals set by the school for the school, ways need to be found to gauge the degree of success in moving towards these. Quality assurance measures assist in this monitoring process.

MANAGEMENT AND QUALITY ASSURANCE

The challenge

In the current political and administrative context schools can be seen as competitive businesses with a workforce, a budget, a service and internal and external clients. The 'new' skills needed have always been in operation but now the major challenge is to harness the individual mission of the school through staff development and support to meet client requirements, maintain a customer base (i.e. keep intake figures up), good reputation and fulfil broader roles with minimum staff stress and within financial bounds.

The business and quality language inevitably intrudes. Undoubtedly the pace of change has hotted up and new managerial responsibilities have surfaced. The head-teacher is not a senior classroom practitioner and instructional leader in the 1990s. Getting to know the pupils, an item in Whitaker's (1983) definition of a primary head-teacher's role, is not now a tenable first-order goal. The Teachers' Pay and Conditions Document (DFE, 1993) determines new roles, e.g. estates manager with the LEA as landlord and the governing body as tenants, and new emphases, e.g. working to policies established by the governing body and evaluating the quality of teaching and learning (insufficiently in evidence according to the HMCI (OFSTED, 1995, p. 23)).

Heads of department also have to resolve the tension between explicit requirements for what to cover and achieve in their subjects and how to liaise with colleagues to manage the broader cross-curricular experiences.

Classroom teachers increasingly need the management skills to organize classroom helpers and classroom assistants (associate staff) and, in their growing responsibility for the holistic development of pupils, the skills to manage relationships with parents, other education professionals and social workers. Schools cannot claim a separateness as a welfare agency which off-loads onto other services difficulties when they arise – 'I'm a teacher, not a social worker' – if only because the school is the location where the pupils develop, manifest their problems and are most accessible for contact.

The response

Clearly senior management in the school has a decisive new role under LMS and even more so under GM arrangements. Balancing budgets, acting as estate manager, taking greater responsibility, with governors, for hiring staff and negotiating pay may consti-tute increments to the role of school managers but they do not make a distinctive enhancement to the education profession.

Organizing quality, targeted staff development, often differentiated (that word again) and individualized, sometimes negotiated, is a centrally important role. It is one means of developing individuals and the institution. It is the means by which a school invests to improve areas of weakness or establish excellence in areas already strong. Staff development is a major way of fulfilling the school mission and promoting movement towards goals of the development plan. Appraisal, school review, inspection, all push towards addressing staff development needs and the school's possession of a staff devel-opment budget facilitates positive response. Five development days, $2\frac{1}{2}$ per cent of the school year, allow sustained collegial approaches to staff development. Day *et al.* (1994), Frost (1995) and Elliott (1993) are amongst the many who underscore the importance of the in-service education of teachers in improving school quality. Much of this should be school-centred, school-managed and be 'corporate' i.e. collegial, managerial and informed by policy. In this continuing development of professional expertise it is important for schools to maintain their links with research and higher education including teacher education centres. To be an entirely practice-oriented enterprise, driven by external political administrative imperatives, would be to render teaching a job for technicians.

A further set of management developments concern involvement with training and mentoring students in initial teacher training, mentoring new staff and managing associate staff. If teachers in schools are to retain a control of the education business, then playing a part in shaping recruits to teaching is a new, developing part of the strategy. The skills of mentoring are not commonplace (Wilkin, 1992) and are not necessarily those which go with the ability to manage the learning of pupils well. Extending the mentoring role to taking responsibility for the care, initiation and development of new staff to the school is also important.

Other adults to be managed by teachers are classroom helpers and classroom assistants (Mortimore and Mortimore, 1994). There has been a big increase in the latter in recent years and there is much that they can do to relieve the teacher to concentrate on the more exacting pedagogical tasks mentioned earlier. These developments will lead to improvements in the quality of provision by the education service.

Senior management, including heads of department in secondary school, need to extend their skills in evaluating the quality of teaching and learning. This may involve classroom observation, questioning pupils and examining their work. Self-monitoring is more important than external inspection (see contributions to Brighouse and Moon, 1995).

Such quality assurance is not just the responsibility of senior staff but of all teachers. Total Quality Management may not be the framework to adopt wholesale (Parsons *et al.*, 1994) but involvement of all personnel in quality assurance matters *is* vital. West-Burnham (1992) and Drummond (1992) both emphasize the collegial philosophy and *that* is what has to be generated and maintained by institutional leaders if educators are to 'get it (nearly) right most of the time', 'work smarter, not harder', 'delight the customer', etc. Quality assurance is not just about achievement in subjects by pupils but about all of the goals the school pursues, including those broader, process and social goals.

The public relations base that this provides is sound. School staff at all levels should be committed and able to present the school to prospective pupils and the public. This can be a genuine communicating process, not just selling, and is part of the school positively demonstrating its self-confidence.

INTERPERSONAL, COMMUNICATION AND RELATIONSHIP SKILLS

Although this section is brief, it is the vital underpinning of the new skills already mentioned. Education and our views about education are greatly affected by our interpersonal transactions with educators which we experience as children and later as adults. Teachers can no longer function covertly in classrooms as though relationships with the immature are all that are important, important though those relationships are. Individually and collectively we are treated as we allow others to treat us. Teachers need a diplomatic, authoritative voice claiming legitimacy on the basis of theory, practice and political mandate for what they do. These abilities need to be nurtured.

'Giving teaching back to the teachers' (Barrow, 1984) will not happen. It will be a matter of 'reclaiming our professionalism' (Ovens, 1995) as the title of the Collabora-

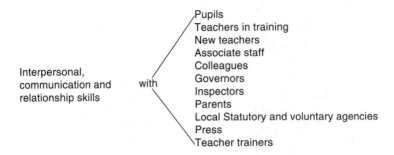

Figure 5.3 *Significant others to whom teachers relate.*

tive Action Research Network conference for 1995 put it. Hargreaves (1994) has argued for a synthesis of professional and institutional development in his discussion of a new professionalism. He subheads sections of his paper 'from individualism to collaboration', 'from hierarchies to teams' and 'from survivalism to empowerment' and these give an idea of the ingredients of his 'post-technocratic' model.

Figure 5.3 sets out the range of people that teachers need to relate to with confidence. Devoting effort to communicating with external audiences, managing trainees, new teachers and associate staff is not time wasted or a detraction from the major task of teaching children. Children, parents and the community (society?) need to feel that the experience of school is legitimate, that it is the proper place for young people to be and that the experiences they have there are important. It makes educating easier if pupils arrive with some aura of the rightness of being there, communicated through parents and press.

NEW SKILLS, NEW SCHOOLS, NEW PROFESSIONALISM

The new skills may not all be so new but together those covered in the earlier sections mark a change in the role of schools and in the nature of teachers' professionalism.

Primary schools have much more to contend with than was previously the case, with increased numbers of pupils recognized as in poverty and in distressed domestic circumstances. Pupils no longer leave secondary school to enter work but go forward, after 16, sometimes in the school, to equip themselves for uncertainties of the future. In part both primary and secondary schools are places of safety away from the perils of violence, crime, sex, drugs and street boredom. That caring role and the provision of a healthy developmental environment is important.

The emphasis of late has been on measured cognitive gains for pupils and the 'effective' school has been seen as an institution getting good examination passes or positively skewed Key Stage National Curriculum Assessment results. That is not the major consideration in a 'good' school. Gammage has proposed that:

> a good school is 'good' not so much because of the specific nature of what is taught (though that is important) but through the manner in which a positive, supportive, richly and frequently interactive atmosphere is developed.
>
> (Gammage, 1985, p. 15)

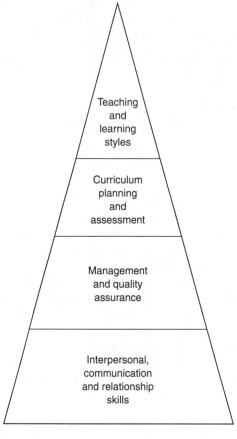

Teaching
and
learning
styles

Active, motivational,
theory-based;
targeted, negotiated,
differentiated;
new technologies.

Curriculum
planning
and
assessment

Auditing, goal-oriented, process-focused;
making the hidden curriculum explicit;
empowering curriculum;
applied diagnostic assessment.

Management
and quality
assurance

Developing and supporting staff;
managing associate staff;
managing relations with public,
community and parents;
business planning;
managing inspectors and inspection;
managing stress and workload;
managing quality self-assessment;
quality improvement.

Interpersonal,
communication
and relationship
skills

Collegial, assertive, communicative,
confident, involved with training and
mentoring, linking with the
community and parents;
non-confrontational relationships with
pupils.

Figure 5.4   *The new skills pyramid.*

Earlier Holtz reminded us:

> We once hoped that schools would create new models of community, encourage new commitments towards meaningful vocations, end racial discrimination, and open up new avenues out of poverty and unhappiness. Right now, it seems, we rejoice if children can be taught to read.

> (Holtz, 1981, p. 300)

Holtz writes as an American and undoubtedly education in the United States is a major force in the anti-poverty drive and is funded at national and state levels to counter drugs, violence, crime and other social ills (Silver, 1994). Effective schools in that country means more than achieving measured cognitive gain. We must strive for that status and that role for education in the United Kingdom. To do that effectively we each need what O'Hanlon has called 'an articulated personal theory' (O'Hanlon, 1993) but we need it on the level of the individual, the institution and the profession.

The new skills pyramid (Fig. 5.4) is intentionally layered in that way with the lower skills being prerequisite for those higher up. The central developments for a new professionalism lie in grasping, and having politically legitimated, a role in a broader social goals oriented curriculum with a theory-based approach to the work. Schooling *is* welfare, though education professionals have colluded in separating themselves from that function. Ribbins (1985) has presented a series of chapters on seeing the role of education in welfare policy and that role needs to be developed with vigour. Best *et al.* (1995) states that 'the commitment of responsible adults to the well-being of children is intrinsically worthwhile and requires no further justification' (p. 291). The remit that education can create for itself can be a more important one than that which it had in the past. The view might be that the state has taken the curriculum and the teaching profession has embraced education, development and caring.

ACKNOWLEDGEMENTS

I wish to thank my colleagues at Canterbury Christ Church College who commented helpfully on an earlier version of this chapter – Sue Capel, Tricia David, David Frost and Jon Nixon.

REFERENCES

Abbotts, R., Birchenough, M. and Steadman, S. (1988) (2nd edn.) *GRIDS – Guidelines for Review and Internal Development in Schools – Primary and Secondary School Versions.* York: Longman.

Balding, J. (1992) *Young People in 1992.* Exeter: University of Exeter.

Ball, S. J. (1994) *Education Reform.* Buckingham: Open University Press.

Barrow, R. (1984) *Giving Teaching Back to the Teachers.* Brighton: Wheatsheaf.

Bennett, N. (1976) *Teaching Styles and Pupil Progress.* London: Open Books.

Best, R., Jarvis, C. and Ribbins, P. (1980) *Perspectives on Pastoral Care.* London: Heinemann.

Best, R., Lang, P., Lodge, C. and Watkins, C. (1995) *Pastoral Care and Personal-Social Education: Entitlement and Provision.* London: Cassell.

Blatchford, P. and Mortimore, P. (1994) 'The issue of class size for young children in schools: what can we learn from research?' *Oxford Review of Education,* **20** (4), 411–28.

Board of Education, Consultative Committee (1926) *The Education of the Adolescent.* London: HMSO.

Board of Education, Consultative Committee (1933) *Infant and Nursery Schools.* London: HMSO.

Brighouse, T. and Moon, B. (eds) (1995) *School Inspection.* Harlow: Longman.

Brown, S. (1990) 'Assessment: A changing practice.' In T. Horton (ed.) *Assessment Debates.* Milton Keynes: Open University Press.

Bruner, J. S. (1986) *Actual Minds, Possible Worlds.* Cambridge, Mass: Harvard University Press.

CACE (Central Advisory Council on Education) (1967) *Children and Their Primary Schools.* London: HMSO (*Plowden Report*).

Carr, W. and Kemmis, S. (1986) *Becoming Critical: Education, Knowledge and Action Research.* Lewes: Falmer.

CIPFA (Chartered Institute of Public Finance and Accountancy) (1993) *Education Statistics 1993–94 Estimates.* London: CIPFA.

Cook, R. (1992) *The Prevention and Management of Stress: A Manual for Teachers.* Harlow: Longman.

Day, C. *et al.* (1994) *Personal Development Planning Nottingham.* University of Nottingham, School of Education.

DES (1987) *National Curriculum Task Group on Assessment and Teaching.* London: Department of Education and Science.

DES (1989a) *The Curriculum from 5–16 (2nd edn. incorporating responses) Curriculum Matters 2.* London: HMSO.

DES (1989b) *Planning for School Development: Advice to Governors, Head Teachers and Teachers*. London: HMSO.

DES (1991) *Development Planning: A Practical Guide*. London: HMSO.

DES (1992) *Curriculum Organisation and Classroom Practice in Primary Schools: A Discussion Paper*. London: Department of Education and Science.

DFE (1993) *School Teachers' Pay and Conditions*. London: HMSO.

DFE (1994) *Pupils with Problems, Circulars 8/94–13/94*. London: Department of Education.

Drummond, H. (1992) *The Quality Movement*. London: Kogan Page.

Elliott-Kemp, J. and Williams, G. L. (1980) *The DION Handbook*. Sheffield: PAVIC Publications.

Elliott, J. (1991) *Action Research for Educational Change*. Milton Keynes: Open University Press.

Elliott, J. (1993) *Reconstructing Teacher Education*. Lewes: Falmer Press.

Frost, D. (1995) 'Integrating systematic enquiry into everyday professional practice: towards some principles of procedure.' *British Educational Research Journal*, **21** (3), pp. 307–22.

Galton, M., Simon, B. and Croll, P. (1980) *Inside the Primary Classroom*. London: Routledge & Kegan Paul.

Gammage, P. (1985) *What is a Good School?* University of Nottingham: National Association for Primary Education, pp. 1–15.

Glasersfeld, E. von (1989) 'Learning as a constructive activity.' In P. Murphy and B. Moon, *Developments in Learning and Assessment*. London: Hodder & Stoughton.

Hargreaves, D. H. (1994) 'The new professionalism: the synthesis of professional and institutional development.' In *Teaching and Teacher Education*, **10** (4), pp. 423–38.

Holtz, B. W. (1981) 'Can schools make a difference?' (Review of M. Rutter *et al*. 'Fifteen thousand hours'). *Teachers College Record*, **8** (2), pp. 300–7.

Hopkins, D. (1990) *TVEI at the Change of Life*. Clevedon: Multilingual Matters.

Hoyle, E. (1988) 'Leadership and Mission.' In R. Glatter, M. Masterton, M. Preedy and C. Riches (eds) *Understanding School Management*. Buckingham: Open University Press.

Jensen, B. B. (ed.) (1995) *Health Education and Democracy*. Copenhagen: The Royal Danish School of Educational Studies.

Kelly, A. V. (1995) *Education and Democracy: Principles and Practices*. London: Paul Chapman.

Lawrence, D. (1988) *Enhancing Self-Esteem in the Classroom*. London: Paul Chapman Publishing.

Lawton, D. (1980) *The Politics of the School Curriculum*. London: Routledge & Kegan Paul.

Lovey, J., Docking, J. and Evans, R. (1993) *Exclusion from School*. London: David Fulton.

Macrae, S., Bliss, J. and Askew, M. (1994) *Deconstructing Scaffolding*. Paper given at the British Educational Research Association Annual Conference, Oxford, September 1994.

Mortimore, P. and Mortimore, J. (1994) *Managing Associate Staff*. London: Paul Chapman Publishing.

Mortimore, P. *et al*. (1988) *School Matters: The Junior Years*. Wells: Open Books.

National Commission on Education (1993) *Learning to Succeed*. London: Heinemann.

NCC (National Curriculum Council) (1990) *Curriculum Guidance 3: The Whole Curriculum*. York: NCC.

OFSTED (1993) *The Handbook for the Inspection of Schools*. London: HMSO.

OFSTED (1995) *The Annual Report of Her Majesty's Chief Inspector of Schools Part I: Standards and Quality in Education 1993/94*. London: HMSO.

O'Hanlon, C. (1993) 'The importance of an articulated theory of personal professional development.' In J. Elliott (ed.) *Reconstructing Teacher Development*. Lewes: Falmer.

O'Keeffe, D. and Stoll, P. (1995) *School Attendance and Truancy*. London: Pitman.

Osborne, A. (1990) 'The nature of educational management.' In B. Davies, L. Ellison, A. Osborne and J. West-Burnham (eds) *Education Management for the 1990s*. Harlow: Longman.

Ovens, P. (1995) 'The conference philosophy.' Paper for the Collaborative Action Research Network (CARN) Annual Conference, 8–10 September 1995.

Parsons, C. (1994) 'The politics and practice of quality.' In C. Parsons (ed.) *Quality Improvement in Education*. London: David Fulton.

Parsons, C., Howlett, K. and Corbett, F. (1994) *Institutional Development Planning*. Lancaster: Framework Press.

Pickles, T. (1992) *Dealing with Disaffection*. London: Longman.

Ribbins, P. (ed.) (1985) *Schooling and Welfare*. Lewes: Falmer Press.

SEAC (School Curriculum and Assessment Authority) (1994) *The National Curriculum and its Assessment: Final Report*. London: SEAC.

Silver, H. (1994) *Good Schools, Effective Schools*. London: Cassell.

Sutton, R. (1991) *Assessment: A Framework for Teachers*. Windsor: NFER–Nelson.

Tate, N. (1995) 'Friends, subjects, citizens ...' *Education Guardian*, 5 September 1995, p. 8.

Tattum, D. *et al.* (1993) *Understanding and Managing Bullying*. Oxford: Heinemann.

Vygotsky, L. S. (1987) *Thought and Language*. Cambridge, Mass: MIT Press.

Waterhouse, P. (1990) *Flexible Learning: An Outline*. Stafford: Network Educational Press.

West-Burnham, J. (1992) *Managing Quality in Schools*. Harlow: Longman.

Whitaker, P. (1983) *The Primary Head*. London: Heinemann.

Wilkin, M. (1992) *Mentoring in Schools*. London: Kogan Page.

Chapter 6

The Need for In-Service Education

Brian Spence

TEACHERS' IN-SERVICE EDUCATION AND TRAINING NEEDS AND THE 1990S

The in-service education and training (INSET) needs of teachers in the 1990s must be appraised against the complex backdrop of change in schools spearheaded by an accelerating process of centrally directed educational reform, begun in the early 1980s and culminating in the 1993 Education Act, which has cast the schools, their headteachers and governing bodies, and the local education authorities (LEAs) in new roles to which they are only now adjusting. Previously acquired pedagogical, classroom management and curriculum development skills have had to be renewed and rethought, while others, of a more entrepreneurial kind and more akin to business affairs, have had to be acquired by those who manage the schools.

Many changes have occurred in the scope, extent of provision, modes of delivery and, not least, in the funding and control of the in-service education and training deemed necessary for a developing teaching profession since the *James Report* (DES, 1972) put INSET firmly on the national education agenda by elaborating first the in-service needs of teachers in the Third Cycle. What has not changed is the need to balance personal and professional development, and to strive to achieve the one through the other, by means of appropriate in-service activities. Moreover, the aspirations for the Third Cycle, expressed in the introduction to the *James Report*, remain pertinent today, namely, that the education and training of teachers could be, and should be, at its best then and that the quality of education and the standards of the profession could be improved speedily, powerfully and economically.

Another need which is by no means new, but which has been thrown into sharper relief as a consequence of recent educational reforms, is the development and sustenance by appropriate INSET strategies of reflective practitioners tentatively defined for the present as teachers who, as an outcome of varying modes of personal and professional development, are enabled to adopt an analytical and critical approach to teaching and learning, to take a dispassionate view of their own and others' part in the process, and who are able to see their roles in a wider institutional management context. The possible consequences for INSET of striving to meet the needs of the 'reflective practitioner' as first elaborated by Schön (1983a; 1983b; 1987), applied to the circumstances of the late 1990s, is given more detailed treatment later in this chapter.

At the heart of the changes wrought by the 1988 Education Reform Act in particular, and the changes to the structure and procedures for school government in the 1980 and 1986 Education Acts, is a major shift in power from the controlling LEA to the semi-autonomous management unit – the self-managing school. A considerable degree of role reversal has accompanied this process, fuelled by the effects of the financial delegation provided for in the 1988 Education Reform Act. The local education authorities have been shorn of many of their former control functions to have them replaced by monitoring, training, advising and enabling ones. These are partly unaccustomed, though important, roles which place the LEAs in a different INSET relationship with their schools than formerly. LEAs are now but one of the providers of in-service resources whose services can be 'bought in' by the schools. The providers of INSET have now truly entered the market-place.

Parallel with that change, and a consequence of it, the individual school has become a unit of 'management' rather than a unit of 'administration'. The headteacher and the governing body are responsible, in partnership, for the management of the material, financial and human resources available to the school, for staffing policy, for staff development, for the definition of the school's INSET needs and for much else besides. Headteachers, whether of primary or secondary schools, have to extend their awareness and concerns to embrace not only long-established educational and development issues such as curriculum renewal, pedagogical updating, classroom management, providing for pupils with special educational needs, timetabling and staff deployment but also monitoring the school's finances, fund-raising, staff appraisal skills and procedures, employment legislation and personnel matters with publicity and marketing. Heads and governors must operate more at the interface between the school and the community than hitherto in order for the school to survive, let alone prosper, in an increasingly competitive market-place in which parents, as consumers and clients, have increasing influence.

A major driving force behind many of the changes just described has been Local Management of Schools (LMS) which, as the Coopers and Lybrand Report (1988) made plain, was intended to have greater impact on the education system and its management than careful financial accounting alone would indicate. Inherent in LMS is a philosophy of management and a redefinition of relationships, as the following extracts indicate:

> The underlying philosophy of financial delegation to schools stems from the application of the principles of good management. Good management requires the identification of management units for which objectives can be set and resources allocated; the unit is then required to manage itself within those resources in a way which seeks to achieve the objectives; the performance of the unit is monitored and the unit is held to account for its performance and the use of funds. These concepts are just as applicable in the public sector as they are in the private sector. (para. 1.5)

> In short, the change at school level is from administration (of centrally determined programmes) to management (of local resources). What is required is a fundamental change in the philosophy of the organisation of education. Thus the changes required in the culture and in the management processes are much wider than purely financial and should be recognised as such. (para. 1.12)

The Secondary Heads Association (SHA, 1990, p. 3) was more explicit in declaring that what was new was the formula distribution of resources in a context which forces schools to make the most effective spending decisions in a manner which ensures that schools compete for the available customers. 'The success or failure of individual schools will lie more than ever before in the hands of the managers – the heads and deputies who form the executive or management team of the school.' The roles of the three parties to LMS were seen as changing significantly in relation to each other. The LEA would take on a more strategic role in setting general objectives for its education service, framing curriculum policies, determining the total resources available to schools, and in providing advice and support. The governing body would control the running of the school within the delegated budget, determine the school's educational needs and priorities, deploy the resources and develop a management plan. The head-teacher, assuming the role of the managing director of a company, would have a key role in advising the governing body, assisting it in formulating the management plan, while securing its implementation with the collective support of the staff.

A major consequence of the institutional change which has accompanied the educa-tional reform process is that the time-honoured partnership between the LEA and its schools, in which the LEA and its advisory staff took a major role in initiating INSET and staff development activities, and in deciding on expenditure, has been significantly eroded. The semi-autonomous management units, which most schools now are, need also to change internally if they are to cope collectively with the management challenges posed by the changes outlined earlier. New internal partnerships of staff at all levels of responsibility, acting in concert with the governing body, are needed. The development of team-working and team-building skills would therefore appear to be both a major means to success and a continuing in-service need. At the same time, the relationship between the school staff as a collectivity and the variety of in-service provision avail-able will need to be redefined if the school is to be helped to function optimally by means of carefully targeted in-service and staff development activities. The latter redef-inition of relationships will form the tentative conclusion to this excursion into the in-service needs of teachers in the 1990s. Further examination of the team ethic is rele-vant here as an aspect of the desirable activity of the reflective practitioner.

The potential benefits of working in teams, both for the individuals who comprise them and the school as a whole, have long been acknowledged by writers on educa-tional management, viz., Marland, 1971; Marland and Hill, 1981; Paisey, 1981; Blackburn, 1983; Donnelly, 1990; Bell, 1992. Teams are perhaps even more pertinent when changes in the predominant management style in the external environment of schools has shifted from management by consensus to management by accountability (Blanchard, Lovell and Ville, 1989). Schools can be evisaged, ideally, as structures consisting of a series of interlocking and mutually supporting teams, led and developed by middle and senior management and co-ordinated and given cohesion by the activities of the headteacher and senior management team.

In a recently published text on managing teams in secondary schools, Bell (1992, pp.1–3) proceeds from two basic premises: that all teachers have a 'direct and develop-ing part' to play in the management of the school at some level and that, as schools do not consist of autonomous individuals acting independently, there is a need for school management to be based on teamwork. Bell also points out that the pay and conditions regulations for standard grade teachers and headteachers alike stress the wider responsi-bilities which involve working with colleagues and accepting a degree of accountability for the work which extends beyond what happens in the individual classroom.

A team is more than a collection of individuals and it is only worthy of the name when it is judged by results and the manner in which its members have interacted in order to achieve specified objectives. As Pipes (1991) asserts heads have, at one and the same time, to manage the senior staff team, in addition to the larger team of the whole staff, and also monitor the development of all other teams in the school. 'Team building and management is therefore one of the key functions of Headship' (Pipes, 1991, p. 2.9–01). The aim is for teams to become 'regenerative' (Pipes, 1991, p.2.9–02), that is, they will now allow their functions to become obsolete while the members acknowledge each other's contribution to the team, set and achieve targets, trust each other, communicate openly and are creative and innovative.

Team leadership often comes from within rather than being imposed from above, while there is a supportive atmosphere within the team; see the description given by the DES (1985) of 'good teachers' at work:

> The members of staff work as a team so that they can offer leadership and guidance in areas of the curriculum that might present difficulties to individual teachers. In this way weaknesses and omissions are assessed and, as far as possible, remedied. These comments emphasise the importance of professional teamwork for maximum curricular strength and mutual support. (paras. 13–30)

Johnston and Pickersgill (1992, pp. 239–48), writing on primary school headship, see the head's role as one of 'team-oriented leadership' in an era of collective responsibility and accountability which requires them to know 'when to take the lead and when to confirm the leadership offered by their colleagues.'

The nurturing of effective work-teams, no mean feat in itself, does not automatically guarantee that all staff will be involved and feel themselves to be members of a particular team and, more importantly, a part of the school operating as a team. As George Thomas's account of the internal changes wrought by the LMS pilot scheme in which his staff was involved demonstrated (Downes, 1991, Ch.3), enhancement of the roles of middle management could be accompanied, on the one hand, by a diminution in the functions of members of the senior management team, and by lack of involvement by staff at departmental level on the other, unless specific measures are taken to guard against that outcome.

A possible measure is provided by Roberts and Ritchie's analysis (1990, pp. 17–21) of the possible consequences for management structures in secondary schools of certain features of the National Curriculum. Traditional hierarchical models of curriculum management are being undermined by the need for cross-curricular planning and the need to manage cross-curricular themes on a whole school basis. A new management structure is called for which sets out clear relationships and encourages flexibility. Roberts and Ritchie propose a 'Battenberg Cake' model which encapsulates a layered system of functions and relationships which they see as necessary to enable senior management to take on a proactive planning and evaluative role.

In this model each dimension of the curriculum, or layer of the cake, e.g. subject curriculum, cross-curricular themes, staff and student services, is 'serviced' by a deputy head and a supporting team. As a means for collaborative management in secondary schools other layers, for example, community service, school–industry links, could be added. What is vital, if the 'reflective practitioner' of the literature is to move from rhetoric to reality, is that the teams should be widely representative of the staff at all levels in a school.

The essential objective of this chapter, while being framed within the context of developments in INSET funding in the 1980s, and an awareness of the implications in turn of central government direction and the devolution of INSET funds to school governing bodies on the determination and prioritizing of INSET needs, and decisions about the most cost-effective means of satisfying them, is not to examine those government initiatives in any detail. Nor is its purpose to pronounce in any exhaustive way on the effectiveness of the different modes of INSET available. Its purpose, by revisiting, examining and updating the concept of the 'reflective practitioner', is to attempt a specification of the INSET needed, and its possible organization, to support the development of such reflective teachers who, acting together, constitute what I shall call the 'reflective school'.

INSET, belatedly, is now the focus of considerable discussion and debate and many questions can be asked. Typically, in a complex activity involving several clients and different providers, the questions are easier to formulate than the answers. My selection of key questions is as follows. The first and last are perhaps the most important in the context of the chosen focus of this chapter.

- What is effective INSET?
- How should effectiveness be evaluated and by whom?
- Who should decide between the different INSET needs (national, local, institutional, individual) which can be identified?
- How do those needs interrelate and how best can they be brought into harmony?

IN-SERVICE EDUCATION AND ITS RELATIONSHIP TO STAFF DEVELOPMENT AND PROFESSIONAL DEVELOPMENT

In-service education and training (INSET) can take different forms in attempting to achieve different objectives and can be the means for the satisfaction of different agendas for bringing about change in education. As Dean (1991) has observed, the terms INSET, professional development and staff development have not infrequently been used synonymously to refer both to the process of individual development and to organizational growth. If INSET is to be relevant to needs then it is to be expected that handbooks on staff development and/or professional development should devote considerable attention to the forms of INSET judged to lead in the desired direction. However, useful distinctions can be made between these closely related terms in order to pinpoint what INSET might potentially contribute to each.

Oldroyd and Hall (1991, pp. 2–3) classify the wide and varied range of INSET activities into three groups as follows:

> *professional education*, by which is meant a widening and deepening of a teacher's theoretical perspectives by means of advanced study;
> *professional training*, the development of knowledge and skills which are of direct applicability to daily work; and
> *professional support*, activities aimed at developing on-the-job experience and performance.

They observe that in recent years changes in the funding arrangements for INSET, and the pressure to implement centrally directed reforms, have placed the emphasis on professional training to the detriment of professional education, while in order to improve teacher performance they propose that more time and money ought to be invested in professional support activities. Given the emphasis on meeting system needs, they use the term 'staff development' to refer to managing those forms of INSET aimed to develop the capacity to satisfy the requirements of the 1988 Education Reform Act, the local education authority, and the school development plan. Staff development, in this formulation, aims at promoting development *for* performance and *of* performance – the training and support roles of INSET. Staff development is, therefore, more orientated towards developing the school than towards developing the profession. Bradley's elaboration of the purposes of staff development (1991, p. 2), and his categorizing of the variety of activities which might contribute to it, focus also on school development while satisfying individual performance and career development needs. By means of enabling people to feel valued in the work they do, and helping them to anticipate and prepare for change, individual teachers might be better able to contribute to school development.

Professional development, on the other hand, is regarded by Oldroyd and Hall, for example, as a more extended concept implying improved control over working conditions, enhanced professional status and career development, and the serving of individual as opposed to system needs. Dean's definition (1991, p. 19) of professional development also gives pre-eminence to the personal or individual dimensions while it does not neglect the organizational relevance of the internalization of acquired knowledge and skills, that is

> Professional development is first of all a matter of the personal development which enables a person to tackle new tasks, relate well to others, see important issues and so on. Part of this development is the acquisition of specific skills, knowledge and understanding, both for the classroom and for management. This knowledge, skill and understanding gradually needs to become internalised and refined so that it becomes part of the teacher's *professional personality* [author's italics] and is available when needed.

Blackman (1989, pp. 1–15) points out that how we view professional development is a direct outcome of the way we view teachers' roles – as appliers of a craft, as classroom isolates, as functionaries or as professionals. Different agendas for professional development will be set depending on the view taken.

Professional development activities focused on the methods and techniques of teaching would seem appropriate to a craft view of a teacher's role. Professional development focused on the classroom activities of the teacher would seem to accord with an isolationist perspective. While, if teachers are seen primarily as the functionaries of the education system, then the managers of the system will take the lead in setting the agenda for professional development, i.e. the establishment of priorities through the successive government training grant schemes in the 1980s.

If, however, we see teachers as professionals, the scope of the issues is widened and the focus is more system-orientated to include decision-making, thinking about practice and professional knowledge over a range of issues wider than the purely pedagogical. Blackman also points out that if we take a more limited view of teachers' roles we will tend to focus on what they can do rather than on what they are and can become. There is, however, even more to it than that as Blackburn (1989, p. 2) explains:

If we view teachers as professionals, we also consider them capable of creating their own agendas for professional development. Thus, as we alter our views of the teacher's role, from that of technician to that of professional, the focus of the agenda for professional development is altered, the locus of concern is broadened, and the sources of the agenda changed. The view of the teacher as professional permits us to get beyond the technologies of teaching to gain a fuller understanding of what we seek to do in schools and why.

While the distinctions made here between staff development and professional development are relevant to selecting the most appropriate INSET means to suit the ends, there is clearly overlap between them and that occurs in the personal growth dimensions of these formulations. Dean's phrase 'professional personality' encapsulates succinctly the desirable end-point of well-designed INSET – a teacher who has achieved understanding by means of study, who has acquired skills by means of various modes of training, who has developed in professional competence from the support provided in and out of school and who can reflect productively on experience in his or her own interests and in those of the school as a whole. In short, what is required is INSET for the 'reflective practitioner'.

THE REFLECTIVE PRACTITIONER RE-VISITED

Donald A. Schön's critique of the shortcomings of the modes of training traditionally pursued by university professional schools (1983a, 1983b, 1987) makes explicit the processes and assumptions which go towards producing the 'reflective practitioner' as a partial corrective. In Schön's analogy (1987, p. 3) of the 'topography of professional practice' a high ground overlooks a swamp. Each locale has defining features which in his analysis call for a rethinking of the priorities of professional training and, at the same time, produce a dilemma for those responsible for its design – a choice between rigour or relevance.

On the high ground the professional problems encountered are manageable and solved through the application of rigorous research-based theory, acquired by means of a normative professional curriculum which gives high status to systematic, preferably scientific, knowledge. The problems of the swampy lowland, by contrast, are ill-defined and defy ready technical solution and can best be approached by 'reflection-in-action', the exercise of the 'competence and artistry already embedded in skillful practice' (1987, preface, p. xi)

The irony is, as Schön points out, that the problems of the high ground, so amenable to solution by means of 'technical rationality', are relatively unimportant to society at large. The problems of the swamp are those of greatest human concern. Schön proposes that the problems of real-world practice, which tend to present themselves as indeterminate situations, should be the point of departure for a new epistemology of practice and professional training. Schön argues that university-based professional schools should learn from traditions of education for practice which emphasize coaching and learning by doing, such as art and design studios, music and dance conservatories, athletics coaching and craft apprenticeship. As Schön puts it, 'professional education should be redesigned to combine the teaching of applied science with coaching in the artistry of reflection-in-action' (1987, p. xii). The reflection-in-action he proposes is constructive and situation-specific. 'Through complementary acts of naming and framing, the practitioner selects things for attention and organises them, guided by an appreciation of the situation that gives it coherence and sets a direction for action' (1987, p. 4). The problematic situations encountered will often present themselves as unique cases which are not amenable to solution by the simple application of rules in the practitioner's store of professional knowledge.

Schön argues from this that a major basis of professional training should be what he calls a 'reflective practicum' whose main features are learning by doing, coaching rather than teaching and a dialogue between coach and student focused on 'reciprocal reflection-in-action' (1987, p. 303). The practicum is 'a setting designed for the task of learning a practice' (1987, p. 37) in which the learner comes to recognize competent practice and, from the learning provided, assimilates the 'practice of the practicum' by means of a combination of learning by doing, and interacting with coaches and fellow learners. The learning and practising takes place under the guidance of senior practitioners e.g. studio masters or supervising physicians who may instruct in a conventional sense but who mainly function as 'coaches' by demonstrating, advising, questioning and criticizing.

Calderhead and Gates in their introduction to *Conceptualising Reflection in Teacher Development* (1993) observe that, 'reflection has come to be widely recognised as a crucial element in the professional growth of teachers.' They suggest that the current enthusiasm for 'reflective teaching' is partly explained by the attempt to understand what is distinctive about teachers' professional development and, at the same time, a reaction against increasing centralization in the control of education which perpetuates a limited view of teachers as technicians or 'deliverers of the curriculum', paralleled perhaps by a 'delivery man' view of INSET as Bradley has dubbed it (1991, p. 82).

The notions of reflection, learning-by-doing, and coaching, seminally expounded by Schön, find distinct resonances in several other formulations of the optimum conditions for effective adult learning and development which I shall argue have direct relevance to the management of INSET for the conditions likely to prevail in the late 1990s. A litany of terms bearing close resemblance to Schön's reflective practitioner reads as follows:

Eric Hoyle's (1973) distinction between the 'restricted' and 'extended' professionalism of teachers in which the former has a high level of classroom competence and teaching skills, while the latter has, in addition, a wider view of teaching in a community and social context and ensures that practice is informed by theory, research and current good practice;

Lawrence Stenhouse's notion of the 'teacher as researcher' (1975) and of the curriculum as a specification about the practice of teaching as opposed to a package of materials or a syllabus requiring ground to be covered;

Sheila Galloway's 'professional model' of INSET (1993), which puts teachers at the centre of the process, assessing and re-assessing their practice alongside colleagues. In principle, Galloway argues, such INSET should result in professional development growing from within the classroom and the school;

M. W. McLoughlin's 'adaptive schools system' (1976) whose main features are proactive responses to external pressures; the stimulation of internal demand for change; multi-level staff participation; and the development of ownership and commitment;

Oldroyd and Hall's 'self-developing school' (1991) which exhibits a coherent and co-ordinated approach to curriculum and staff management and to general school management and organization. Such a school is characterized by a high level of collaboration and an active senior management team. Oldroyd and Hall present four related images – the enabling LEA; the self-developing school; the collaborative team; and the reflective teacher;

Holly and McLoughlin's 'new professional' (1989) which marks the shift from 'teacher-as-information dispenser' to 'teacher-as-researcher';

Howard Bradley's notion of 'the design team' (1991) in the process of bringing about effective change in schools, accompanied by professional development.

INSET, whose effectiveness can be judged by the extent it brings about the development of teachers, depends on how bringing about change is conceived – as directed from above or as the outcome of teachers' active development of it. In the latter scenario teachers are the members of a design team keeping ideas flowing.

ACTION RESEARCH MODELS OF TEACHER BEHAVIOUR AND DEVELOPMENT

Models of action research in schools use similar language in characterizing professional development and behaviour and have in them an implicit 'practicum', as Schön would have it. The essence of action research has been encapsulated as the study of a social situation with a view to improving the quality of action within it (Elliott, 1991). Altrichter, Posch and Somekh (1993, p. 5) see action research as supporting teachers in coping with the challenges and problems of carrying through innovations in a reflective way and suggest that the current period of change in education presents an opportunity to build a dynamic culture of teaching and learning in schools. They see action research as a facilitator of professionalism as it involves positive change via 'reflective rationality'. Action research, similar to Schön's 'practicum' assumes that complex problems demand specific solutions, that those solutions can be developed only within the context in which the problem exists, and that the solutions, while situation specific, are communicable to other practitioners. Very similar assumptions were made by Day (1981), namely that teachers' development can only come from themselves, that effective learning occurs in response to 'real' questions posed by the learner and that decisions about teaching should stem from reflection on previous actions. Carr and Kemmis (1986) see in action research self-reflective inquiry which is undertaken by participants in social situations with a view to understanding practice and the situations in which it is carried out. The process is envisaged, in a school improvement context, as a self-reflective spiral of cycles of planning, acting, observing and reflecting.

This revisiting of the notion of the reflective practitioner indicates both its durability and its currency as an ideal to be sought, in this case by means of appropriate INSET leading to staff development which meets both individual and institutional needs. Major questions remain:

- How can we recognize reflective practitioners when we meet them?
- Are particular modes of INSET more or less likely to lead in the desired direction?
- How can the development of such teachers be nurtured in conditions which can

fairly be described as innovation overload?

Calderhead and Gates (1993, p. 2) indicate that teacher education programmes based on notions of reflective practice can be based on one or more of the following list of aims:

- to enable teachers to analyse, discuss, evaluate and change their own practice, adopting an analytical approach towards teaching;
- to foster teachers' appreciation of the social and political contexts in which they work, helping teachers to recognise that teaching is socially and politically situated and that the teacher's task involves an appreciation and analysis of that context;
- to enable teachers to appraise the moral and ethical issues implicit in classroom practices, including the critical examination of their own beliefs about good teaching;
- to encourage teachers to take greater responsibility for their own professional growth and to acquire some degree of professional autonomy;
- to facilitate teachers' development of their own theories of educational practice, understanding and developing a principled basis for their own classroom work;
- to empower teachers so that they may better influence future directions in education and take a more active role in educational decision-making.

Closer inspection of the list reveals a major initial emphasis on 'ownership' in references to 'own practice', 'own beliefs about good teaching', 'own professional growth', and 'own theories of educational practice'. However, the egocentrism, if such it can be called, is couched in a wider social and political context, perhaps empowering teachers to act together. The total agenda is educational and 'political' in its references to professional autonomy and participation in decision-making, the latter perhaps beyond the confines of the teachers' immediate work situation. That is a formidable agenda for any stage in the development of teachers and could be problematic for initial training if only for lack of sufficient experience to reflect upon. While the process of reflection might begin in initial training it is in in-service education that measures can be taken to nurture and support reflection.

Dilemmas abound for those who would wish to promote teacher reflection. Two are particularly relevant to in-service education. These are the integration of knowledge that arises from reflection on practice with theoretical knowledge, and the issue of whether reflection is an individual or a collective pursuit. In the latter case the individual nature of reflection on practice is often stressed, while there is some evidence (Zeichner and Liston, 1987) that a supportive environment fosters it. Both are relevant to the school-based in-service practicum proposed here in which the development of reflective practice is targeted at the whole school rather than at particular individuals.

Russell's (1993) elaboration of the possible critical attributes of a reflective teacher can perhaps help us answer the questions posed earlier concerning the recognition and nurturing of reflective teachers. Russell posed several questions concerning the observable behaviour of reflective teachers which can clarify the search for the in-service education most likely to lead in the desired direction.

In an in-service context the key questions Russell poses would seem to be the following:

- How does a teacher know when reflection is productive?
- Is a teacher who can articulate principles of practice being reflective?
- Does being reflective mean thinking about one's teaching, or does it also require doing something about one's teaching?

Russell's answer to the first question is 'reflection is productive when it leads to changes in practice that may or may not be retained but result in a better personal understanding of one's practice' (1993, p. 146). His answer to the second question, aware of the often significant gap between belief and action, is 'Yes', provided the principles of practice match the practice rather than one's personal beliefs about it.

It is, however, his answer to the third question, informed by an interest in Schön's 'reflection-in-action', which is perhaps most important for the future shape of in-service education. Russell concludes, 'being reflective serves little purpose if it does not involve, in central and essential ways, changes to teaching as well as development of thinking about teaching' (1993, p. 147).

MODELS OF IN-SERVICE EDUCATION AND TRAINING

The ideal characteristics of the reflective teacher, just indicated, bear resemblance to Oldroyd and Hall's formulation (1991, Ch. 2) of the characteristics of well-directed staff development and their model of the types of INSET activity needed to engender and support it. They argue that, when teachers are asked to behave differently, they must change in four ways – in what they know, in what they believe, in what they are able to do and in what they actually do. INSET is needed for knowledge, skills and performance. It is, however, the dynamic links between those three purposes which are important in determining the structure and provision likely to provide for the needs of the reflective practitioner. Activities designed to enhance performance provide the means for linking competence, the ability to do something, with performance. In Oldroyd and Hall's analysis beliefs change through a combined process of action and reflection and are likely to be affected by professional dialogue based on feedback about performance.

A distinction can, therefore, be made between professional training and professional support whose components provide the basis for the distinction between Type A and Type B INSET activities proposed in Oldroyd and Hall's model, namely:

> *Type A* (Professional training) which consists primarily of received learning 'delivered' by experts through courses or workshop activities of varying durations. These could be provided by higher education institutions or the LEA, or a combination of both, and could be school-based, both in terms of the location of the expertise and the target clientele.
> *Type B* (Professional support) which is primarily concerned with learning which is acquired on the job, perhaps with the support of colleagues or a trainer or consultant. In the process of teaching or managing the practitioner is given opportunity to reflect while 'in action' and 'on action' individually or with support and feedback from colleagues.

Oldroyd and Hall contend that effective staff development will take account of the best features of both types of in-service education and avoid the pitfalls which each on its own can entail. Type A INSET is usually provided 'off-site' and, therefore, has the potential advantage of widening the individual participant's perspectives. Hence, for example, short 1–2 day courses with a specific focus, longer 20-day courses with a wider training and development brief, and long award-bearing secondments can provide a much needed corrective to the risk of insularity which could be encouraged by Type B activities alone. However, ensuring a transfer of the training so acquired to the daily work of the course participant, which needs to be internalized and practised in order to 'take', is difficult to ensure without the internal support which Type B INSET can provide.

A common-sense conclusion would be, as Oldroyd and Hall acknowledge, to regard both types as mutually supporting. The task of the leadership in primary and secondary schools of the headteacher, senior management team and the staff development co-ordinator, is, therefore, to attempt to achieve a judicious blend of INSET activities designed to satisfy and harmonize clearly defined individual and institutional in-service needs.

INSET AND CLASSROOM PRACTICE

The effect of in-service education on classroom practice is inevitably a concern of those who fund it, provide it and receive it. The problem as Burgess and Galloway express it (1993, p. 169) is stark in its simplicity:

> If the prime purpose of INSET is improved quality of teaching there is still relatively little systematic evidence on the extent to which INSET affects classroom practice. Though impact in the classroom is said to be the acid test of INSET, the paradox is that it can be very difficult to identify.

In attempting to identify positive ways forward in evaluating the effect of INSET on classroom practice they indicate both the importance of the question to DFE, the LEAs and the schools for whom, variously, it represents an investment of funds, time and effort for which a return is sought, and the methodological dilemmas facing those who would attempt to measure the effectiveness of INSET provision. In the latter connection, self-reporting, questionnaires, interviewing teachers about their classroom practices, systematic observation of classroom practice before and after a particular in-service experience, qualitative methods, 'illuminative' evaluation and triangulation using a range of techniques all compete for a place in the process, and most have shortcomings when they are used in isolation.

Paradoxically, as HMI acknowledge (DES, 1991), the 'quality' of the particular INSET experience is not the sole criterion of impact – the state of 'receptivity' of the participant and of the school can also be significant:

> However, neither good management, a good course, or the motivation of the participants is, in isolation, a sufficient condition for INSET to have an impact. There is evidence that highly motivated teachers can take back something valuable from an indifferent course, just as there are very stimulating courses which leave certain participants quite unmoved. The influence of a good course well matched to participants' needs may be frustrated by resistance or apathy within the school when the recently motivated teacher returns.

Ongoing research by Richard English at the University of Hull into bringing about change in the mathematics classroom poses the question whether INSET initiates change of merely supports it. While teachers could identify in-service training as being responsible for some changes, other factors, such as the National Curriculum and its associated assessment procedures and the examination boards, were considered to be of greater importance. English (1995) identified also a primary/secondary divide in the extent to which in-service training was identified as a change factor, a feature which has been noted in other research, e.g. Halpin, Croll and Redman (1990); Kinder, Harland and Wootton (1991). Perhaps primary schools are more able to create an environment characterized by a whole-school approach to in-service training needs fully supported by the headteacher.

Among Burgess and Galloway's suggestions for ways forward (1993, p. 173) to relating in-service training to classroom practice and researching its contribution more effectively is to take steps to develop further the ability to 'think evaluatively', part of the 'stock-in-trade' of all teachers, to document the process and make it visible as a part of professional learning. INSET for the reflective school should therefore attempt to take account of the optimum conditions for initiating change and supporting it but also take account of how teachers learn.

TEACHERS AS LEARNERS

Perhaps a well-articulated sequence of learning such as that proposed by Joyce and Showers (1980) which proceeds from the presentation of theory, through demonstration of skills, practice and feedback, to coaching for application, is an inappropriate model of teachers' learning on-the-job. Dean (1991, pp. 19–20) comments that, while that sequence might have validity for initial teacher training, the process tends to be more haphazard later when learning might take place, for example, through trying out an idea to address a particular problem, or comparing notes with a colleague.

For Dean (1991) and Oldroyd and Hall (1991), learning is best rooted in experience and collaboration as exemplified in TRIST (Technical and Vocational Education Initiative Related In-Service Training For Teachers) funded in-service developments in which, among other things, teachers pool their expertise, approach common problems, are offered tested strategies to tackle those problems and are offered cases of existing good practice as exemplars. Oldroyd and Hall (1991, p. 33) quote the example of how TRIST funding moved a school from staff development based on *ad hoc* and piecemeal personal development, through an emphasis on collaborative development which stimulated some in-house INSET, to a focus on collegial development where TRIST funding was used to move from patchy collaboration to a systematic assessment of individual and institutional needs.

David Kolb's exposition of 'experiential learning' (1984) provides insight into the kind of learning well-directed in-service training might call for and also develop. Experiential learning, as expounded by Kolb, has its roots in Lewin's model of action research in which the here-and-now is used to test abstract concepts; in Dewey's conception of learning as a process of integrating experience and concepts, observations and action; and in Piaget's notion of learning as an interaction between the individual and the environment, involving the accommodation of concepts to experience and the assimilation of events into existing concepts. Expressed graphically by Kolb (1984, p. 38) 'learning is the process whereby knowledge is created through the transformation of experience.'

Kolb proposes that learners need four different kinds of abilities if they are to be effective – concrete experience abilities, reflective observation abilities, abstract conceptualization abilities and active experimentation abilities. If possessed in equal measure by teachers these should enable them, in turn, to become fully involved in new experiences, to reflect upon and observe those experiences from several viewpoints, to create concepts which integrate those observations into theories and to use those theories to aid decision-making and problem-solving.

IN-SERVICE EDUCATION FOR THE REFLECTIVE SCHOOL

The in-service training arrangements needed to assist the development of reflective practitioners who, collectively, might constitute the 'reflective school' do not call for new modes of INSET delivery *per se*, nor for teachers to do essentially different things when engaged in their training and development from what they did in the past. Still less do they call for the schools to make an exclusive choice between Type A and Type B INSET activities as they have been elaborated by Oldroyd and Hall. What is required is support for reflection in and on action, and a strucure to facilitate it, which, while acknowledging the uniqueness of each school, and the realities of the financial constraints which have determined that more and more INSET will be school-based and school-focused, avoids isolationism and attempts a judicious blend between carefully diagnosed individual and institutional needs.

I propose, therefore, that each school as an entity should be regarded, in Schön's terms, as a 'reflective practicum' which both initiates inquiry and plays an initial role in developing staff by such means as coaching in skills from senior staff or those with special expertise, observation and feedback, and action research projects. To facilitate the development of the 'practicum' a new partnership is suggested, parallel to the close collegial relationships which are now a feature of the more firmly school-based arrangements for initial teacher training. Each school, or a cluster of primary schools, for example, should have an 'in-service mentor', for want of a better word, from a higher education providing institution, who would work in close collaboration with the staff development co-ordinator, the headteacher, senior management team and the staff as a whole in order to develop a whole-school approach to staff development and related in-service activities.

Among the in-service mentor's roles would be those of consultant and change agent assisting the school's management to maintain and develop the practicum and to lend support in building and maintaining the team which is, and should be, the whole school. Other possible roles would consist in providing assistance in diagnosing in-service needs, in helping to formulate the staff development and in-service annual plan and rolling programme which would aim to achieve a balance of relevant in-school and out-of-school activities, and to act as a critical friend in evaluating school-based action research/staff development activities.

By these means it should be possible to achieve the integration of knowledge gained from reflection on practice with theoretical knowledge which so exercised Schön's attention and also ensure that in-service activities are well matched to needs, which would seem to be a major element in effectiveness. Were this to be done then perhaps INSET providers could more readily satisfy the training needs of secondary school heads, deputies and governing body chairs expressed in a recently reported research project carried out under the auspices of the UBI NEPU (Understanding British Industry National Education Programmes Unit) with the support of Unilever, OFSTED and DFE (DFE, 1995). The needs of all three groups were revealed as generic in character, involving, for example, strategic management; monitoring, evaluation and review; development strategies; and working with the school management team. Providers might also be placed in a better position to respond to the messages to which the project team wished to draw their attention among which were to obtain and respond to client feedback, to monitor their own performance and publicize their findings, to keep costs under constant review, to provide for needs country-wide and to respond flexibly to the needs of individual schools.

REFERENCES

Altrichter, H., Posch, P. and Somekh, B. (1993) *Teachers Investigate Their Work*. London: Routledge.

Bell, L. (1992) *Managing Teams in Secondary Schools*. London: Routledge.

Blackburn, K. (1983) *Head of House, Head of Year*. London: Heinemann.

Blackman, C. A. (1989) 'Issues in professional development: the continuing agenda'. In M. L. Holly and C. S. McLoughlin *Perspectives on Teachers' Professional Development*, pp. 1–15. London: Falmer.

Blanchard, T., Lovell, B. and Ville, N. (1989) *Managing Finance in Schools*. London: Cassell.

Bradley, H. (1991) *Staff Development*. London: Falmer.

Burgess, R. G., Connor, J., Galloway, S., Morrison, M. and Newton, M. (1993) *Implementing In-Service Education and Training*. London: Falmer.

Burgess, R. G. and Galloway, S. (1993) 'Epilogue: does in-service education have an effect on classroom practice?' In R. G. Burgess, *et al. Implementing In-Service Education and Training*, pp. 168–73. London: Falmer.

Calderhead, J. and Gates, P. (eds) (1993) *Conceptualising Reflection in Teacher Development*. London: Falmer.

Carr, W. and Kemmis, S. (1986) *Becoming Critical*. Lewes: Falmer.

Coopers and Lybrand (1988) *Local Management of Schools. A Report to the DES*. London: HMSO.

Day, C. W. (1981) *Classroom-based In-Service Teacher Education. The Development and Evaluation of a Client-Centred Model*. University of Sussex, Education Area Occasional Paper, No. 9.

Dean, J. (1991) *Professional Development in School*. Milton Keynes: Open University Press.

DES (1972) *Teacher Education and Training (The James Report)*. London: HMSO.

DES (1985) *Education Observed 3: Good Teachers*. London: HMSO.

DES (1991) *Implementation of the Local Education Authority Training Grants Scheme, 1988–1990*. DES 53/91/NS, para. 58, p. 14.

DFE/OFSTED (1995) *Summary Report. Developing Senior Management*. London: HMSO.

Donnelly, J. (1990) *Middle Managers in Schools and Colleges. A Handbook for Heads of Department*. London: Kogan Page.

Downes, P. (ed.) (1991) *Local Financial Management in Schools*. London: Blackwell.

Elliott, J. (1991) *Action Research for Educational Change*. Milton Keynes: Open University Press.

English, R. W. (1995) 'Are secondary headteachers losing touch?' *British Journal of In-Service Education*, **21** (1), 1–9.

Galloway, S. (1993) 'Identifying INSET needs.' In Burgess, *et al. Implementing In-Service Education and Training*, pp. 88–112. London: Falmer.

Halpin, D., Croll, P. and Redman, K. (1990) 'Teachers' perceptions of the effects of in-service education.' *British Educational Research Journal*, **16** (2), 163–77.

Holly, M. L. and McLoughlin, C. S. (1989) *Perspectives on Teachers' Professional Development*. London: Falmer.

Hoyle, E. (1973) 'Strategies of curriculum change.' In R. Watkins (ed.) *In-Service Training; Structure and Content*, pp. 91–103. London: Ward Lock Educational.

Johnston, J. and Pickersgill, S. (1992) 'Personal and interpersonal aspects of effective team-oriented headship in the primary school.' *Educational Management and Administration*, **20** (4).

Joyce, B. and Showers, B. (1980) 'Improving in-service training: the message of research.' *Educational Leadership*, **37** (5), 379–85.

Kinder, K. and Harland, J. (1991) *The Impact of INSET; The Case of Primary Science*. Slough: NFER.

Kinder, K., Harland, J. and Wootton, M. (1991) *The Impact of School-Focused INSET on Classroom Practice*. Slough: NFER.

Kolb, D. A. (1984) *Experiential Learning; Experience as the Source of Learning Development*, pp. 20–38. Englewood Cliffs: Prentice-Hall.

McLoughlin, M. W. (1976) 'Implementation as mutual adaptation change in classroom organization.' *Teacher's College Record*, **77** (3), 339–51.

Marland, M. (1971) *Head of Department*. London: Heinemann.

Marland, M. and Hill, S. (1981) *Departmental Management*. London: Heinemann.

Oldroyd, D. and Hall, V. (1991) *Managing Staff Development. A Handbook for Secondary Schools*. London: Paul Chapman Publishing.

Paisey, A. (1981) *Organisation and Management in Schools*. London: Longman.

Pipes, M. (ed.) (1991) *NAHT Guide to School Management*. London: Longman.

Roberts, B. and Ritchie, H. (1990) 'Management structures in secondary schools.' *Educational Management and Administration*, **18** (3).

Russell, T. (1993) 'Critical attributes of a reflective teacher; is agreement possible?' In J. Calderhead and P. Gates (eds) *Conceptualising Reflection in Teacher Development*, pp. 144–53. London: Falmer.

Schön, D. A. (1983a) *The Reflective Practitioner*. London: Temple Smith.

Schön, D. A. (1983b) *How Professionals Think in Action*. New York: Basic Books.

Schön, D. A. (1987) *Educating the Reflective Practitioner. Toward a New Design for Teaching and Learning in the Professions*. San Francisco: Jossey-Bass.

SHA (Secondary Heads Association) (1990) *Managing the Money*, p. 3. London: MAPS(SHA) Ltd.

Stenhouse, L. (1975) *An Introduction to Curriculum Research and Development*. London: Heinemann Educational.

Zeichner, K. M. and Liston, D. P. (1987) 'Teaching student teachers to reflect.' *Harvard Educational Review*, **57**, 23–48.

Chapter 7

Role Clarity

Ron Best

INTRODUCTION

> Teaching ... can perhaps best be described as an act of ambivalent faith. Remove the faith and all that remains is ambivalence. Faiths may vary but I'm sure that they are central to commitment and that commitment is a vital part of the ability to execute the job with the dedication that the children and school deserve. Headship and teaching require all or nothing; there is no room for half measures, for limited commitments. My faith is of a quite simple nature and rests on my imperfect knowledge of children's capabilities. Their limitations relate to our limitations as teachers; given time and good teaching they can produce work of beauty and insight, skill and complexity. Knowing that, I must work towards the possibility of each child attaining his or her full potential. I work within the realities of the school and of its teachers which will mean compromise; it will mean patience but with faith anything may be possible. Faith overcomes the petty problems, the daily frustrations; it is the anchorage.
>
> Ambivalence represents confusion. The nature of that ambiguity varies. The decisions of when to intervene; the need, on occasions, to be authoritarian; the need for information to be shared, yet confidences to be respected. The constant tension between the need to act and the time to consider. If only these dilemmas remain and faith is gone or denied its place then the job becomes intolerable for there is no substance remaining.
>
> (Stone, 1989, p. 4)

This statement, written by a primary school headteacher in 1989, strikes me as an excellent summary of what many teachers feel, though rarely articulate with such clarity. Stone is expressing a fundamental tension between on the one hand, a clarity of personal commitment to the mission of the teacher, and on the other, the uncertainty, ambiguity, ambivalence and dilemma with which the teacher's daily work is unendingly beset. Stone is clear about her commitment and she writes with a certain moral authority. She accepts that a degree of ambiguity and incoherence is inescapable in the teacher's role, and can live with it provided her personal ideology of education provides a firm anchorage.

It is significant that she wrote this statement in 1989, for the Education Reform Act of the previous year marked a watershed in the developing pattern of state-provided education. For a role which perhaps already lacks some of the clarity of comparable roles in other caring professions, the changes which have taken place in education since the mid-1980s and which culminated in 1988 and all that, have contributed to the complexity and on occasions incoherence of the role, and to many teachers' feelings of ambivalence about it.

Stone continues: 'my equilibrium is profoundly disturbed by the current educational legislation. It seems that it will deny my faith' (Stone, 1989, p. 5). To pursue the metaphor, she is by no means alone in finding her anchorage to be drifting. On the contrary, few teachers have been untouched by the events of recent years.

This chapter examines the need for clarity in the role of the teacher. It argues that the complexity and diffuseness inherent in the role is exacerbated by contemporary changes in the organization and politics of education, and suggests some ways in which greater role clarity might be secured.

ROLE AND ROLE CLARITY

Sociology has given us two distinctive ways of thinking about role. In the first (associated with the 'structural functionalist' or 'systems' paradigm) roles are seen as sets of expectations which attach to status positions in social systems. Thus, the role of the teacher is the socially expected behaviour attached to anyone who fills the status position 'teacher' in our society. In the second (associated with the 'symbolic interactionist' and 'phenomenological' paradigms), roles are socially constructed products of interactions between individuals with personal aspirations and institutional responsibilities.

The concept of *expectations* is common to both definitions of role. The difference lies in the degree to which the role incumbent is perceived as the passive respondent to the expectations of other roles (and of society at large), and the degree to which he or she is considered to be proactive in shaping and developing her/his performance such that the expectations of (first) significant and (second) generalized others with whom he or she interacts are the outcome and not the determinant of social interaction. It is the classic tension between individual freedom and initiative on the one hand, and social constraint and conformity on the other, of role-*taking* versus role-*making* (Turner, 1969). An understanding of teachers' work requires a recognition of both moments of this dialectic. It is not the case that individuals exclusively perform the role of teacher by mechanically following some generalized and consensual set of social expectations; nor are they entirely free agents in determining what teachers' work is. Stone's 'faith and ambivalence' is born of the inescapable fact that teachers live their lives in the net of tensions and dilemmas which is generated by the coexistence of freedom and constraint in all human experience.

One thing which all schools share is a certain vagueness about the overall aims and objectives of education. Underpinning the rationale for socially organized education ('schooling') is some concept of the 'educated person'. The philosophers of education of the 1960s (Peters, Hirst, Oakshott *et al.*) were much concerned with this idea. Linked to it was some assumption about the nature of civilized or educated society. While some teachers (like Stone above) may feel very clear about their mission, it is not at all clear what society expects of schools. The education system performs several social functions, including acting as a mechanism for selection for broad occupational strata and the social status which accompanies them, the development of productive human talent for the economy and the promotion of patriotism and national loyalty.

The current debate about the relative merit of A Levels, GNVQs, NVQs, GCSEs and so on demonstrates a long-standing dispute about the relationship between liberal education and vocational training as legitimate aims for schooling (Pring, 1993). At the same time, schools struggling to interpret OFSTED and NCC guidance on moral, social and spiritual development are very aware of the lack of precision about educational aims. Those who castigate schools and teachers for producing youth who participate in football violence, drug taking, 'raves' and so on, do so on the basis of a concept of civilized behaviour derived rather narrowly from their own. In short, what teachers ought to do is very much a matter of opinion, and that opinion depends upon the social, cultural and biographical details of the individual who advances it. In so far as there is a consensus about this, I fear it is at the level of simple generalities: that teachers should teach the children something called 'knowledge' and control their behaviour.

One source of tension for teachers is the *diffuseness* of the role itself. Hargreaves (1972) summarized many attempts to identify and list the sub-roles which comprise teaching. The sheer number of such roles – fount of knowledge, parent substitute, police officer, judge, resource manager, assessor, evaluator, instructor, etc. – ensures that expectations lack precision, and vary widely, and that teachers' efforts to play such diverse roles leaves the role expectations diluted and fuzzy. Hargreaves was led to conclude that the core of the role was to be found in just two of its dimensions: that of 'instructor' (the transmission of knowledge and the promotion of learning) and that of the 'disciplinarian' (the control and management of behaviour). Yet as we have already noted, this is radically to simplify the complexity and variability of the work which teachers do.

Even if Hargreaves is correct in identifying the disciplinarian and the instructor as the core sub-roles teachers play, it does not follow that even these sub-roles are especially clear. On the contrary, both are the subject of ongoing debate as to what is required of the 'good' teacher.

It is now generally recognized that the orthodox dichotomy of 'formal-traditional' and 'informal-progressive' (or 'child-centred') teachers is too simplistic. As theoretical ideal-type models they continue to have some (limited) use. But it is clear from research over many years that teachers tend to adopt wide-ranging and not always strictly compatible attitudes to different aspects of their role and are prone to vary their approach according to circumstances (Galton *et al.*, 1980).

Teachers may be bewildered, therefore, to find reports from sources which are more or less 'official' appearing to emphasize one rather than the other of these classic ideal-types. The emphasis given to subject knowledge, whole-class teaching and the importance of 'the basics' in the 'Three Wise Men' report (Alexander *et al.*, 1992), or the emphasis in the Elton Report (1989) on behavioural management (rather than on pastoral care, counselling and the diagnosis of behavioural patterns) suggests that their authors are adopting the formal-traditional perspective. In a similar way, the conception of the National Curriculum as programmes of study with specified content and measurable outcomes originates in a 'transmission' model of teaching in which the teacher is active, the pupil passive and the processes inside the child a 'black box' about which relatively little is known. It is significant, perhaps, that *by law* the Secretary of State cannot direct teachers in the methods which they are to use nor schools in the procedures they are to adopt in planning and delivering the curriculum (Watkins, 1995, p.

125), but there is much in NCC guidance documents and elsewhere which may be read between the lines. To the teacher who is struggling to meet the National Curriculum requirements, examples of possible approaches are likely to be seen as having the force of prescription.

That said, there are clearly other prescriptions around. It is part of what Ball (1990) has termed the 'discourse of derision' that many of the ills of education are attributable to the child-centred theories of education which were alleged to be prevalent in teacher-training colleges in the 1960s and 1970s – and (one hears) remain prevalent today. In my experience the presence of extreme child-centredness and associated radicalism in teacher education has always been overstated. None the less, in so far as ITE programmes typically seek to promote *positive* discipline and the analysis and diagnosis of behavioural needs, and tend to emphasize social constructivist and cognitive develop-mentalist models of learning rather than behaviourist ones, there is some truth in the charge. Few college tutors would deny or apologize for it; but equally few would recognize the caricature of informal-progressive methods so often presented in the tabloid press and all too often quoted by politicians.

Within the instructional role, clarity of expectation would require that we know a great deal more than we currently do about how children learn. The choice seems to be between competing paradigms which consist in mutually exclusive conceptual frame-works derived from fundamentally incompatible axioms (Kuhn, 1962). One may plump (it seems) for Piaget/Kolhlberg, Bruner/Vygotsky or (possibly) Donaldson, or settle for a pragmatic but strictly speaking contradictory eclecticism (see Pollard, 1990). The prior question – what counts as *evidence* that a child has learned something and under-stood it in the way we empathically come to believe she or he has – remains so difficult that opting for one explanatory framework rather than another remains something of an act of faith.

The point is that on issues such as whether to stream or not to stream, whether to use group methods or whole-class teaching, or whether retributive punishment or 'community service' is more likely to be effective, there is no consensus. Ideal-types may help the NQT to understand something of the variety of available styles upon which to model her/his own approach, but precisely how one should play each of these basic sub-roles is, if anything, less clear than in the past.

Another source of tension is in the *ambiguity* of the role. Writing about organizations in general, Handy (1985, p. 61) says that

> the four most frequently cited instances of role ambiguity in a work situation are:
>
> Uncertainty about how one's work is evaluated;
> Uncertainty about scope for advancement;
> Uncertainty about scope of responsibility;
> Uncertainty about others' expectations of one's performance.

It requires little reflection to concede that these uncertainties are present to a greater or lesser extent in the roles which many teachers play. Handy goes on to comment that such ambiguity 'can cause insecurity, lack of confidence, irritation and even anger' amongst those with whom one interacts (the 'role-set') (Handy, 1985, p. 61).

In addition to role ambiguity, teachers experience more or less *role conflict*. This may happen when their performance of the teacher role is in conflict with their perfor-mance of other roles (e.g. mother, parent), or when there is an incompatibility between a number of sub-roles within the teacher's role (e.g. the teacher as disciplinarian and the teacher as counsellor). These are usually distinguished as inter- and intra-role conflicts (Grace, 1972, p. 3). Because of its diffuseness, and because of the large role-set (governors, pupils, parents, colleagues, inspectors, LEA officers, etc.), the role of the teacher seems to me to be particularly prone to both types of role conflict.

Handy (1985) identifies two further types of role conflict which he calls *role overload* and *role underload*. In the former (which is not to be confused with *work* overload), the sheer number of sub-roles is so great that meeting the subtly different expectations of all of them becomes impossible. In the latter, the role is so narrowly defined as to permit the incumbent little room to develop the role in interesting and fulfilling ways. Teachers would appear to be prone more to overload than to underload, although in small schools with a stable staff and strong traditional authority, it is possible for 'junior' staff to find themselves locked into a single, strongly framed set of duties.

The effect of these different conditions – role ambiguity, role diffuseness, role conflict, role overload and role underload – upon the individual is usually described as *role stress* or *role strain*. The difference between these is that role stress may be positive in providing motivation and challenge ('role pressure') whereas role strain is debilitating. Handy asserts that individuals suffering from role strain exhibit the following symptoms:

> *Tension.* Often expressed by irritation, excessive preoccupation with trivia, great attention to precision, or periods of sickness. Tension focuses attention on the immediate, polarizes situations into 'black' and 'white' extremes, leads to stereotyped responses and increases sensitivity to rumours and group pressures.
>
> *Low morale.* Often expressed as low confidence in the organization, expressions of dissatisfaction with the job, or a sense of futility.
>
> *Communication difficulties.* Often the individual is hard to talk with or even breaks off communication entirely. He becomes silent and withdrawn. Absenteeism is an extreme form of this symptom.
>
> (Handy, 1985, pp. 65–6)

While it does not follow that role strain is the only explanation for these symptoms, teacher stress seems to be associated with the complexity of the teacher's work as much as it does with the sheer volume of it (Calderwood, 1989). In extreme cases, levels of stress associated with role strain of one sort or another account for seriously impaired functioning leading to 'burn-out' (Vernon, 1987).

INSTITUTIONAL CONTEXTS

When we apply these concepts to education, we need to recognize that the institutional contexts in which teachers work vary considerably, and thus the types of role strain which teachers will experience also vary.

Writing in the context of Further Education, Peeke (1980) reminds us that each role is subject to *three* separate sets of perceptions: that of the occupant of the role, that of the others with whom he or she interacts and that of the 'organisation': that is to say, the *ascribed* role as articulated in the job description, and located in the 'hierarchy of accountability' (Peeke, 1980, p. 77). At least in principle such hierarchies should be designed for the maximally efficient attainment of the institution's goals in ways which are consonant with the prevailing organizational culture.

A feature of secondary education is the existence of often complex bureaucratic structures of roles which institutionalize the major dimensions of teachers' work. In a series of articles published over many years, we have elaborated a model of schools' provision which identifies the *curricular*, *pastoral*, *disciplinary* and *management* roles as encompassing all that teachers do (Best and Lang, 1994, p. 215). The typical secondary school will have devised structures of hierarchical posts of responsibility which correspond to these dimensions, and which may well have built in all manner of potential conflicts for the incumbents. For example, what is often described as the 'pastoral-academic split' or the 'pastoral-academic divide' is a consequence of identifying sub-roles in ways which may cause duplication of effort, uncertainty over responsibilities and sometimes unwieldy lines of communication and referral (Best *et al.*, 1983).

Where formal structures are less clear, there develops what Pollard has called 'institutional bias': sets of negotiated understandings which reflect power differentials and 'which determine many of the routines and practices of the institution' (Nias, 1989, p. 44). Formal structures and 'institutional bias' will vary from sector to sector, and among institutions within any sector. However, successful role performance in such contexts is only partially dependent upon the correct interpretation of formal systems of job descriptions. As any teacher will attest who, when new to the school, committed the great sin of sitting in someone else's staffroom chair, it also requires the incumbent to 'suss out' the norms and folkways of the institutional culture, to 'read between the lines' with due regard to custom and tradition!

Primary schools do not typically have the elaborate formal structures of the comprehensive school. Although there may be some specialization (e.g. the named person for special needs and child abuse or curriculum leaders for the various National Curriculum programmes of study) even in large schools the conventional secondary divisions by subject, faculty, department, year and so on are not to be found. Arguably, primary teachers may thus avoid certain sources of role proliferation but fall prey to others, not least a lack of clarity about expectations in the context of role overload. Recent research by Nias (1989) shows primary teachers' roles to be highly complex and diffuse, and it seems that clarity about the role requires an understanding of, and familiarity with, the idiosyncratic culture (or 'institutional bias') of the school in question.

BOUNDARIES

A major source of role conflict arises from the lack of clarity about the *boundaries* of teachers' roles. There are some matters on which there is a consensus as to what is expected of the teachers: that they should teach the children something, that they should maintain a reasonably orderly environment, prepare children for examinations, assess children's performance and so on. But there are other matters which might be said to lie at the periphery of what is expected of teachers: for example, the behaviour of children once they have left the school premises, the constraints they may place on children's activities at home (how much homework *can* a teacher set?), teachers' right to information about children other than that which directly affects their progress in the curriculum and their behaviour in class.

The British education system has long been premised upon the principle of the teacher *in loco parentis*, but this is less easy to interpret in practice than is commonly realized. Consider the following two descriptions of teachers working at the margins of the recognized role. Both are taken from research interviews undertaken by the author in 1991 (see Best and Curran, 1995).

The case of 'Helen'

Helen's mother died some four years ago when Helen was seven years of age. In the teacher's words Helen 'could not cope'. She would break down in school if anything happened to spark this off. For example, on one occasion a clergyman spoke to the school in assembly about a funeral he had been to. Helen became distraught. On this and other occasions the teacher would have Helen sit on her lap while she wept. These incidents would be followed by periods of depression. The other children in the class knew about Helen's bereavement and made allowances for her.

These upsets would occur about twice a month. In the teacher's view some of these were latterly linked with the onset of menstruation, but others were not. A reference to Mothers' Day was enough to spark a period of tearfulness. The teacher reports that she talked to this child a lot on these occasions, and that a bond developed between them. When the teacher had trapped a nerve in her back and could not brush her own hair, she would allow Helen to brush it for her.

Helen's younger sister is now in this teacher's class. Although too young to remember her mother's death, the teacher wonders if there is not some effect on her also. The child reports having bad dreams. No relationship like that with Helen has developed, however.

The case of 'Toby'

Toby was 8 years old and lived with his mother. For some time he had been refusing to attend school. There had been frequent stomach aches, headaches and other apparently 'phantom' illnesses, but more recently he had been throwing tantrums and becoming violent whenever his mother insisted he go to school. His absences became more frequent and more prolonged.

The Educational Welfare Officer was alerted, and made several visits to the child's home and to the school. She was of the opinion that there was nothing physically wrong with the child, and did not consider this to be a case of genuine 'school phobia'; that is to say, Toby's reluctance to attend school was not a symptom of genuine panic attacks or irrational fear. She advised the head and the mother to take a strong line and simply insist that he attend school.

One morning the mother rang the school to say that she could not bring Toby to school as he had locked them both in the house and hidden the key. The head agreed to drive to the house and see if he could persuade Toby to say where the key was and unlock the door.

Upon arrival, he could see both Toby and his mother through an open downstairs window. Seeing the head getting out of the car, Toby launched a barrage of punches and kicks at his mother. The head climbed in through the window and restrained the child, who eventually disclosed the whereabouts of the key (it was in his pocket!) and agreed to accompany the head to school provided he could take his teddy bear with him. This was agreed, and, face saved, Toby began to attend regularly without further problems.

In neither case is the child able to benefit to the fullest from its schooling until important barriers have been moved out of the way. *Prima facie* Helen's teacher has a right (and perhaps an obligation) to provide the emotional support necessary to allow Helen to benefit from the curriculum. But has she gone beyond what is expected (and acceptable) in the teacher's role by cuddling Helen when she is distressed? And what of the intimacy involved when she allows Helen to brush her hair every morning? As for the head, Toby's attendance at school is compulsory by law, but does this give him the right to enter the house and physically restrain the child, even at the invitation of the mother? And if he had physically forced the child into the car and back to school, how is this to be interpreted: as reasonable force within the head's authority *in loco parentis*, or as an occasion of physical assault?

Teachers may have a legal as well as a professional and moral obligation to act to promote the child's welfare, and this may entail on occasions restraining the child from acts which are harmful to it. But not everyone by any means would agree that the actions of these teachers, however well intentioned, fall within what is clearly the teacher's role.

The boundaries between the different sub-roles which teachers play are similarly vague, and there may be significant role conflict as a result. The teacher who tries to combine the roles of behavioural manager, counsellor and teacher of (say) maths may encounter great difficulties when confronted with the same child in all three roles! The need to impose obedience in order to get through the lesson may make the non-judgemental relationship of the counsellor–client impossible. It is difficult enough for parents to punish and support at the same time; for the teacher who is in all other respects a stranger, this must be a great deal more so.

CHANGE

When roles change rapidly and substantially, this has obvious implications for the clarity with which those roles are perceived by both the role incumbent and members of the role-set. It is arguable that in the last two decades, the role of the teacher in most (if not all) sectors of UK education has been subject to unprecedented change.

As early as 1980, Peeke observed that the role of the lecturer in further education institutions was being changed dramatically. In his particular field (Business Studies), the advent of the Business Education Council (BEC) was a considerable catalyst for change. Amongst the shifts in role which Peeke identified were:

1. A shift from a specialist role to a generalist one;
2. A shift from didactic teaching to student-centred learning through the medium of work-related assignments. This involves a change in the lecturer's conception of the educational process and in the role of the student;
3. A shift towards team teaching and subject integration due to the inclusion of cross-modular assignments in the course programme;

4. A shift from summative assessment to continuous assessment on the basis of assignments performance.

(Peeke, 1980, p. 79)

Since then, of course, there have been further reorganizations as BEC and its technician-training equivalent (TEC) metamorphosed into B/TEC, and the Manpower Services Commission (MSC) emerged to rival the right of the (then) Department of Education and Science (DES) to define education in all spheres. The publication of the MSC's *New Training Initiative* in 1981 introduced to many the new orientation of courses towards competences, a change which has echoed down through the education system as far as the nursery school. As Peeke observes, such changes are by no means unproblematic and some conflict is predictable, not least because 'the new role model willl be subject to lack of clarity and competing expectations' (Peeke, 1980, p. 80).

Comparable changes (and comparable role strain) may be observed in higher education. Parker (1994) researched the attitudes of academics in departments of continuing education in the 'old' universities, and found that the aspects of their roles which they find most rewarding are those aspects of the role which are becoming less prominent in their daily work. Although their vocational and professional interests centred on creative and intellectual work, the increasing requirements of public accountability seem certain to increase the administrative, accounting and marketing dimensions of their roles – precisely those duties which they find *least* rewarding! This perception is one which would be repeated in many other fields of higher education. The tighter links between the inspection, assessment and appraisal of institutions of higher education by such bodies as the Higher Education Quality Council (HEQC), and student quotas, funding for capital investment and research have raised duties concerned with accountability and quality control dramatically in the profile of lecturers' responsibilities.

In teacher education, the successive DES/DFE Circulars (notably Circulars 3/84, 24/89, 9/92 and 14/93), which created the (now) defunct Council for the Accreditation of Teacher Education (CATE), increased dramatically the power of the Secretary of State to determine the requirements of teacher-education courses and specified time allocations for school experience and key curriculum components (notably science and maths). It is arguable that the threat of OFSTED inspections, the knock-on effect on teacher-education of the creation of a National Curriculum in schools and the linking (real or perceived) of quality ratings with the distribution by the new Teacher Training Agency (TTA) of student quotas has created a 'quality-assurance and accountability culture' in which tutors' pedagogic and supportive roles are taking second place to preparation for inspection. One has only to follow the *Letters* and *Comment* sections of *The Times Higher Education Supplement* to realize how bewildering such changes are for those whose conception of the role of the lecturer remains that of the 'don'.

Of course change has been nowhere more obvious, complex and persistent than in the primary and secondary sectors. It goes without saying that the revisions associated with the 1988 Education Reform Act have been comprehensive, rapid and extensive. The advent of the National Curriculum and its associated assessment procedures, and the successive revisions to the programmes of study, SATs and teacher assessments have occupied teachers up and down the country for the last seven years. However, there have been knock-on effects from other aspects of the legislation, and from associated government policy throughout this whole period. The radical changes made to the powers of Local Education Authorities, the delegation of budgets to schools under

LMS, the creation of City Technology Colleges, the reconstitution of school governing bodies and the promotion of 'parent power' have all impacted upon the ways teachers' work is seen. For most of the decade preceding the 1988 Act, change was also part of the normal life of the school. The promotion of curriculum reforms originating with the Schools Council and its successors, the trend towards the integration of children with Special Educational Needs as advocated by the Warnock Report of 1987 and implemented in the 1981 Education Act, the Technical and Vocational Education Initiative (TVEI) and its extension (TVEE), the advent of GCSE and the national system of Records of Achievement were all significant changes during this period.

Under such a barrage of change, it is predictable that teachers will feel the strain. Each change entails at the least a revision of the priorities given to the different sub-roles teachers play, and at most a significant redefinition of the role as a whole (Dunning, 1993).

Primary teachers report a major increase in the amount of 'paperwork' associated with their role, with the National Curriculum being primarily to blame. In a recent case-study of a junior school, one teacher observed:

> What's been the most noticeable thing is the amount of paperwork there is now. To a large extent you are doing exactly the same thing, but you spend so long trying to find out what attainment target is that?

Another said:

> [There is] so much paperwork ... with the National Curriculum ... [you have constantly] to go back to the National Curriculum to make sure you cover the set things ... the paperwork really seems to have taken over.'
>
> (Best and Curran, 1995, pp. 21–2)

Teachers talked at some length about the increase in the amount of preparation, marking and record-keeping which they now have to do at home because the working day is already overfilled with paperwork.

Secondary teachers in a parallel case-study undertaken in 1991–92 made similar comments. Many of the staff interviewed spoke about aspects of the National Curriculum and its associated assessments. At the time, the full impact of the National Curriculum was yet to be felt in some subjects and in later years. For some staff, it had yet to become an issue; for some it merely confirmed changes which were already in train; for others some relatively minor changes in approach and content of their subject were required within the established curriculum. The major impacts for those most fully affected were in the systems of recording and reporting progress which departments had to devise or revise, and the forced dismantling of integrated subjects like Humanities and the ditching of locally agreed syllabuses. Seen at its worst by one teacher, the National Curriculum was 'a mess ... a crippler'. The headteacher described the workload as 'incredible' while several of his staff talked about the increase in the number of meetings, the volume of administration and the amount of reading to be done (Best, 1994, pp. 176–7).

In both the primary and secondary case-studies, teachers identified the *pace* of change to be as significant as the sheer number of changes. The typical view was that 'the goalposts keep moving' to such an extent that teachers 'cannot now expect to do the same thing two years running' (Best, 1994, p. 176).

Not surprisingly, teachers perceived their stress levels to have increased dramatically.

Clearly, some of this stress is to do with work overload; some with role overload as such sub-roles as student profiler, public relations officer and special needs co-ordinator are added to the already considerable array of teacher duties. Some stress is also clearly attributable *per se* to the anxiety and uncertainty of functioning in an environment of constant and accelerating change. It is quite impossible for roles to remain clear and unambiguous under such circumstances.

Casualties in all this have been those roles which are not directly and obviously to do with the delivery of the curriculum. Thus, teachers in the junior case-study described how their provision of lunch-time and after-school clubs and sporting activities had declined in the face of mounting National Curriculum requirements. Both primary and secondary teachers suggested that their pastoral care roles had suffered for the same reason. Thus, secondary teachers argued that pastoral work was 'no longer important on the agenda', that 'teachers have less time for the pupils as individuals because of the pressures of change, including the growing burden of assessment' and that the emphasis on the curriculum meant that pastoral work was no longer a significant criterion for career advancement (Best, 1994, p. 177). As one primary teacher summed up: 'there certainly isn't time for caring so much' (Best and Curran, 1995, p. 22).

ROLE CONGRUENCE AND PERSONAL INTEGRITY

Pastoral care is a particularly good exemplar of role conflict and unclarity because it follows directly from the notion of the teacher *in loco parentis* yet remains an area about which teachers (and schools) are often ambivalent. It is also an aspect of teachers' work which highlights the fact that teaching is a *role* and that those who perform this role play a great many other roles in their daily lives. Teachers experience strain between the expectations of their teaching role and the expectations of such roles as parent, brother, daughter, church-goer, sportsperson, gardener and so on. But they are also human beings to whom there is a great deal more than the total of all the roles they play.

It follows that there may be serious tension between the sorts of things a person may be expected to do as a teacher, and *the sort of person he or she thinks she or he is*. So, if someone's self-concept is that of a warm, caring and supportive person, sensitive to the feelings and personal dispositions of others, yet in playing the role of the teacher she finds herself having to 'harden her heart' to the feelings and needs of one child in order to deliver the curriculum effectively to the others, this has serious consequences.

We may use the concept of *congruence* to describe the relationship between the role and the person. In the above example, there is incongruence since the role expectations are at odds with the self-concept. To remain with this example, there are four possible responses: the teacher revises her view of the sort of person she is ('I'm no longer kind, warm, supportive and sensitive to the feelings and dispositions of others'); she maintains her self-concept but fails to fulfil the requirements of the role; she meets the expectations of the role and rationalizes the incongruence; or she meets the expectations of the role, maintains her self-concept but suffers guilt and anxiety because of the mismatch. Clearly, whichever course she follows is problematic. She may gain public esteem but lose her self-respect; she may retain her self-respect while losing public esteem (and possibly her job!), or she may cease to be a caring person. In any case, she is faced with a crisis of identity.

I am suggesting that a major source of *unclarity* in the role of the teacher is the result of our failure to take seriously into account the degree of congruence between the role and the person. No amount of analysis may remove a certain incongruence, but if the nature of these tensions can at least be recognized and clarified, appropriate support may be offered (Lodge *et al.*, 1992).

MEETING THE NEED FOR ROLE CLARITY

It is clearly important for the individual who takes on the role of the teacher that there should be as much clarity as possible about the role(s) he or she is expected to play. It is also important for the smooth functioning of the school as an organization. As Handy reminds us:

> many of the problems in organizations arise from role strain, misconceptions about role, role underload, or bad communications because of false role expectations
> (Handy, 1985, p. 91)

A school cannot be expected to fulfil its mission if mutual expectations are not clear, if the boundaries of sub-roles and the relationships between sub-roles are not apparent, or if the channels of communication between role-holders are blocked by the 'noise' of fuzzy or incompatible job descriptions.

However, I have been at pains to point out that some unclarity of roles is inescapable for teachers because some tension and contradiction is inherent in the social functions of schooling and, therefore, in the global roles of teachers. To educate or to train? To promote the fullest development of the individual as a moral and rationally autonomous citizen, or to perform a refined selection process for the labour market? To foster freedom of thought and action or to maximize the social integration of conforming and obedient workers? Moreover, we have seen that the boundaries of the teacher's role (and the sub-roles which comprise it) are necessarily blurred in the UK where the teacher is expected to act *in loco parentis*. By definition, to share with the parent a responsibility for the development and well-being of the whole child (rather than for empty heads to be filled with curriculum knowledge) invites debate about where the teacher's responsibility ends. Finally, it is incontestable that the scale and rate of change within the education system in recent years – and there are indications of further change to come – has put teacher's roles in a state of permanent flux.

That is not to say that those responsible for education and schools can do nothing to promote greater clarity about teachers' work. On the contrary, there is much that can be done.

The fundamental debate about the nature and purpose of education is by nature not something which can ever be finally resolved. However, at national and local levels, clearer policies about the relative weight to be given to the educational and training functions of schooling would help, as would some rationalization (now promised) of the academic and vocational qualifications towards which youngsters might work. Some slowing down of the rate of change in the curriculum has now been achieved through the revisions of the National Curriculum requirements under Sir Ron Dearing and this is rightly to be welcomed. However, it is arguable that comparable action is needed in other spheres of educational change in order to allow the new conceptions of teachers' roles to be consolidated and their implications for the role incumbents to be fully worked through.

At school level, there are a number of things which might be done to help teachers cope. These include:

- the full involvement of all staff in the regular review and revision of job descriptions, to include procedures of accountability and channels of communication. This should not be another form of appraisal, and should be undertaken as a natural part of the ongoing and routine evaluation of the school as an organization. (For an example of this idea in practice, see Busher, 1988);
- improved and systematic programmes for the induction of NQTs into the role structure and organizational culture of the school;
- programmes of induction for staff internally promoted or 'moved sideways' to take on roles new to them. There is currently little planned preparation for staff to take on new roles, as (for example) when promoted to middle management positions;
- using staff development days or comparable opportunities to explore the nature of roles and problems of role conflict, ambiguity, congruence and so on. As Handy (1985, p. 91) observes: 'Often, discussion of the problem in terms of role theory clarifies it out of existence';
- recognizing that teachers have lives outside school, and that their role performance is seriously affected by competing demands from other quarters;
- promoting a culture of 'collegiality' (as Hargreaves, 1994, p. 97 *et passim* has called it), in which the relationships between staff are mutually supportive, extend beyond the technical-rational matters of effective task-performance towards an awareness of others' *personal* needs. (For a discussion of the support teachers need based on this recognition, see Lodge *et al.*, 1992.)

One particular matter which remains outstanding is the question of the tension between the teacher as role-*taker* and role-*maker*. One aspect of collegiality is that the staff of the school collaborate in generating aims and objectives as well as devising the plans and strategies by which they may be pursued. There is a phenomenological emphasis here on teachers' roles being the *outcome* of the collaborative interaction which takes place rather than determining interaction through formal role expectations. How realistic is such a view?

At the time of writing, the UK education system has been through a period of unprecedented change characterized by an extensive rhetoric (but less extensive reality) of devolution (LMS; the Parents' Charter; the reform of school governing bodies; etc.) side by side with a significant centralization of control through expanded powers for the Secretary of State, the imposition of a National Curriculum and the creation of a great many powerful quangos (SCAA; OFSTED; the Teacher Training Agency; etc.). While schools are still free to determine how the curriculum is organized and the methods by which it is 'delivered', they do so within what is felt to be a tighter set of constraints than hitherto. The realm within which teachers may exercise their personal initiative and professional judgement has been seriously restricted. The loosening of some of the bonds of the National Curriculum under Dearing has redressed the balance a little, but room for movement remains constrained.

Under these circumstances, the role of the teacher cannot be other than stressful. It may be that what is expected of teachers is clarified by this curious combination of centralism and corporate devolution, but if it is, it is at the cost of teacher autonomy and personal integrity. The concept of a teaching *profession* is seriously compromised, and the incongruence of role with self-concept may be terminal in the 'burnt-out' teacher (Vernon, 1987). On the other hand, if teachers are accorded a greater respect and professional freedom of action, then they will need to relearn their capacity for role-making within a collegial culture. Ambivalence will be inescapable, but as the primary headteacher with whom this chapter began observes, one can live with ambivalence provided one's faith in the mission of teaching is left intact.

REFERENCES

Alexander, R., Rose, J. and Woodhead, C. (1992) *Curriculum Organization and Classroom Practice in Primary Schools*. London: DES.

Ball, S. (1990) *Politics and Policy Making in Education*. London: Routledge.

Best, R. (1994) 'Teachers' supportive roles in a secondary school: a case-study and discussion.' *Support for Learning*, **9**(4), 171–8.

Best, R. and Curran, C. (1995) *The Caring Teacher in the Junior School*. London: Roehampton Institute Faculty of Education. CEDARR Occasional Paper No 1.

Best, R. and Lang, P. (1994) 'Training needs in an international context.' In P. Lang, R. Best and A. Lichtenberg (eds) *Caring for Children*. London: Cassell, pp. 207–16.

Best, R., Ribbins, P., Jarvis, C. and Oddy, D. (1983) *Education and Care*. London: Heinemann.

Busher, H. (1988) 'Reducing role overload for a head of department: a rationale for fostering staff development.' *School Organization*, **8**(1), 99–103.

Calderwood, D. (1989) Some implications of role conflict and role ambiguity as stressors in a comprehensive school.' *School Organization*, **9**(3), 311–14.

Dunning, G. (1993) 'Managing the small primary school: the problem role of the teaching head.' *Educational Management and Administration*, **21**(2), 78–89.

Elton Report (1989) *Discipline in Schools*. Report of the Commission of Enquiry chaired by Lord Elton. London: DES/HMSO.

Galton, M., Simon, B. and Croll, P. (1980) *Inside the Primary Classroom*. London: Routledge.

Grace, G. (1972) *Role Conflict and the Teacher*. London: Routledge.

Handy, C. (1985) *Understanding Organizations*. Harmondsworth: Penguin (3rd edn).

Hargreaves, A. (1994) *Changing Teachers, Changing Times*. London: Cassell.

Hargreaves, D. H. (1972) *Interpersonal Relations and Education*. London: Routledge.

Kuhn, T. S. (1962) *The Structure of Scientific Revolutions*. Chicago: University Press.

Lodge, C., McLoughlin, C. and Best, R. (1992) 'Organizing pastoral support for teachers: some comments and a model.' *Pastoral Care in Education*, **10**(2), 7–12.

Manpower Services Commission (1981) *A New Training Initiative: Agenda for Action*. London: HMSO.

Nias, J. (1989) *Primary Teachers Talking*. London: Routledge.

Parker, S. (1994) 'Changing times, changing roles?' *International Journal of Lifelong Education*, **13**(1), 57–63.

Peeke, G. (1980) 'Role strain in the further education college.' *The Vocational Aspects of Education*, **XXXII**(83), 77–80.

Pollard, A. (1990) *Learning in Primary Schools*. London: Cassell.

Pring, R. (1993) 'Liberal education and vocational preparation.' In R. Barrow and J. White (eds) *Beyond Liberal Education: Essays in Honour of Paul Hirst*. London: Routledge, pp. 49–78.

Stone, C. (1989) 'All that remains is ambivalence: a headteacher's reflections.' *Education 3–13*, October, pp. 4–9.

Turner, R. H. (1969) 'Role-taking: process versus conformity.' In A. R. Lindesmith and A. L. Strauss (eds) *Readings in Social Psychology*. New York: Holt Rinehart and Winston, pp. 215–30.

Vernon, M. (1987) 'A burnt-out case.' In T. Booth and D. Coulby (eds) *Producing and Reducing*

Disaffection. Milton Keynes: Open University Press.

Warnock Report (1978) *Special Educational Needs*. Report of the Committee of Enquiry into the Education of Handicapped Children and Young People, chaired by Mary Warnock. Cmnd 7121. London: HMSO.

Watkins, C. (1995) 'Personal-social education and the whole curriculum.' In R. Best, P. Lang, C. Lodge and C. Watkins (eds) *Pastoral Care and Personal-Social Education: Entitlement and Provision*. London: Cassell.

Chapter 8

The Need to Maintain Morale: A Moral Issue

Mick McManus

'A fire always boosts morale, and it helps to get you noticed. Light a fire' (pilot's advice on surviving a crash landing). Consider these facts taken from newspaper reports in 1994/5: professional competence is at such a low level that the chances of receiving appropriate attention are described as a lottery; half of the most common professional activities are described by experts as useless; dishonesty is so rife that in 1994 there were almost 20,000 complaints involving a total of £30 million; and inflated qualifications and fictitious degrees are commonplace (*The Times*, 25 October 1994, 1 March 1995, 22 October 1994, 29 March 1995).

One would not expect morale to be high in any profession where such major defects are identified – and yet it is. The reports refer, respectively, to the activities of doctors, solicitors and senior managers. In 1994, 100 firms of solicitors were investigated on suspicion of defrauding the legal aid fund: we can only wonder why this and other outrages involving high-status professions are not the subject of daily speeches and questions in Parliament. It is easy to imagine the outcry that would greet such a statistic if it applied to schools, and impossible to imagine that it could be true.

Let's begin again. Consider these facts: in primary and secondary schools teaching is at least satisfactory in up to 80 per cent of lessons, and competence is judged to be good or very good in more than one lesson in three; pupils' standards of achievement and examination results improve every year; in nine out of ten schools teachers manage pupils' behaviour well; and in the overwhelming majority of schools financial control is sound. These facts come from the annual report of the Chief Inspector of Schools (OFSTED, 1995). Plenty to celebrate there, and with such achievements, morale should be high – and yet it does not seem to be. The proportion of unsuccessful lessons (though relatively low) tends to be emphasized, and rising examination successes are dismissed as evidence of examinations getting easier.

Disparagement of teachers and diminution of their self-esteem is a vice of the English-speaking countries. In Britain it reaches comic heights: when three school boys robbed a building society during the school lunch break, and were said to have boasted of their exploit with impunity, the judge explained (to what must have been a stunned courtroom) that 'No amount of modern teaching methods are of any value if a school is unable to instil a basic sense of right and wrong in pupils' (*The Times*, 10 Sept. 1994). The only comment worth making here is that reserving the judiciary to Oxbridge-educated, ex-public school boys is of no value if a QC can make two grammatical errors in one sentence.

Even those who are trying to be nice to teachers manage to be nasty: in 1991 *Encyclopedia Britannica* teamed up with *Woman's Own* to seek the Teacher of the Year; the leaflet asked readers if they knew a teacher whose work, effort, dedication and commitment went beyond the demands of the job and therefore *set them apart* from their colleagues. Moving to the USA one might wonder which of the country's many ills a 1970s' government report entitled *A Nation at Risk* might be about: drugs, crime, the Mafia, race relations, gun-ownership, foreign policy? It was about teaching.

Something must be different about the teaching profession to make its successes something to be despised or suspected and its weaknesses so dwelt upon. There is certainly something different about teachers. To illustrate this difference, consider these responses to a question put to a group of teachers. They were asked what part, if any, moral issues had in their daily work. Without a pause to consider there was a rush to respond positively: 'I think you do it all the time. I think you actually do it throughout your teaching'; 'I deal with moral and social education as they arise, and I will deal with them at the expense of curriculum (technology) as far as I'm concerned'; 'Every minute of a lesson or out on the corridor or taking pupils you are having conversations with them ... (with ethical implications) ... we are doing it all the time with our pupils'; 'I think you are constantly teaching them for life' (McManus and Metcalfe, article in preparation).

We might wonder which other people, professional or otherwise would answer so readily and in this way. Anecdotal evidence from meetings with groups of parents prior to school inspections under the Office for Standards in Education (OFSTED) framework suggests that we do not think about values at all. When asked, in accordance with the agenda, if they are happy with the values the school teaches, they tend to appear nonplussed and have to be prompted. In one case (and this was a group of educated parents) there was a silence; and then they began complaining about pupils smoking on the buses.

When a sample of teachers on in-service courses and staff development days was asked to suggest how morale might be improved, the respondents overwhelmingly indicated two related areas for action: the attitude of those outside schools – society, parents, politicians; and the support available within schools to cope with such things as paperwork and problem children. Of the sample of 133 teachers, 84 per cent mentioned within-school support. For example: 'adequate finance to deliver the goods'; 'better resources and counselling'; 'a trained and qualified person in each school for pupils and staff'; 'a good support system for staff and training to cope with insolent children'; 'time to cope with the paperwork'. More (68 per cent) thought that disruptive pupils contributed to the low morale of other teacher-colleagues than for themselves (38 per cent).

As many as 67 per cent mentioned external attitudes. For example: 'affirmation by society'; 'I would like to be listened to respectfully and have my professionalism recognized'; 'freedom from government posturing'; 'a non-union professional organization that would put forward views for the good of the profession and would have the clout to affect government'; 'recognition from everyone that my job is important, and takes high level expert knowledge.' A total of 63 per cent gave examples of both aspects: 'I work hard to help my pupils achieve their potential and I try to make them feel that they are good and valued individuals and I would love to have some of that done for me. I regard self-esteem as important to pupils and would like my own to be protected. I want to be *esteemed*.' Other responses not clearly falling into these two categories included the desire for higher pay or for a special interest to be respected (children with particular needs, for example).

THE WISH TO BE ESTEEMED

There is irony in this wish of course. If those outside schools and in other professions are as incompetent and dishonest as the reports I began with indicate, their esteem is unlikely to be forthcoming and worth nothing if it were so to be. Perhaps we should reflect on what is probably a major difference between teachers and others, and that is their attitude to basic values. Teaching is suffused with values and the need to be forever setting an example and doing good. Readers might take a moment here to reflect on the characteristics of any good teacher known to them and consider what those characteristics are. They will almost certainly have in mind such things as enthusiasm, approachability, patience and understanding. One author (King, 1978) says that teachers have to be professionally pleasant. These are all personal qualities – not skills or types of subject knowledge – and they turn up whenever I put this question to groups of teachers, whether in primary or secondary schools, selective independents, or urban high schools on deprived estates. They are not characteristics we would list if asked what made a good doctor or lawyer: in these, perhaps, we would be looking for technical expertise as a first priority.

STRESS CONTROL AS A PROFESSIONAL VIRTUE

'If a teacher teaches and the pupils do not understand, he should not become angry with them but should repeat and be prepared to teach his lesson 400 times. A short-tempered person should not become a teacher' (Maimonides, twelfth-century Jewish philosopher).

In the light of these moral and personal features of the teaching role, it is not surprising that those who reject our efforts to teach them are able to cause us so much distress: for if our qualities as a teacher are so much bound up with our qualities as a person, it is likely that we feel rejection of our teaching as rejection of ourselves. Teaching is a vocation in a way that perhaps few other professions are, and its accomplishment is more akin to success in personal relationships than success in a technical craft. Teachers are closer to priests than they may think.

As it is rare for any society to hold teachers in high regard, the contribution that social prestige could make to educational success must remain unknown. Interestingly, the Jewish community seems to be a notable exception, and ample support for the reverence to be accorded teachers can be found in Jewish literature (Angyalfi, 1994). For example, Jacob, on hearing that his lost son Joseph was alive in Egypt, sent Judah ahead to found a school; cities that did not maintain schools might be destroyed; teachers are described as stars upon the firmament of mankind and the true guardians of the city; neighbours were even forbidden to protest about the noise of pupils chanting their lessons in a school. This ancient world is some distance, temporally and morally, from the one in which an English Local Authority recently served a noise abatement order on a playgroup. There is much to be said in favour of studying ancient texts as a means of enhancing spiritual, moral and religious development – and teachers' morale. In the Book of Daniel (12:3) we find: 'Those who have taught many people to do what is right will shine like the stars forever.' If that is not compensation enough, in 1 Timothy (5:17) the advice is that 'Those who do well at the labour of preaching and teaching should be reckoned worthy of double stipend': a level of performance-related pay worth working for. A restoration of the attitudes to teachers prevalent in Biblical literature is overdue.

Government interventions in British education have tried, or seemed to have been trying, to eliminate the human (and humane?) aspect of education. Although the National Curriculum might appear to be a teacher-proof and pupil-proof impersonal catalogue that could be programmed into a computer, there is plenty of evidence that those who actually contributed to it (as opposed to policy-makers) never saw it that way. The National Curriculum Council (NCC, 1989) commented, in relation to pupils with special needs, that 'some pupils meet attitudes and practices in schools which do not actively encourage full participation' and that there was a need for 'positive attitudes from school staff who are determined to ensure their fullest participation.' Guidance on managing pupils with special needs in English warns of an overemphasis on behaviour management 'without attempts to understand the child's feelings'. In a DfE-commissioned contribution to school discipline (Gillborn *et al.*, 1993) we find teachers who have been successful in trying circumstances emphasizing the importance of relationships in their work. Says one of those interviewed: 'All other things come later.' Good teachers must have moral qualities as well as competences.

Those responsible for the training of new teachers have to have regard for what appears to be an impersonal list of competences (DfE, 1992). However, they cannot be attained by trainee-teachers unless they satisfy the twin requirements of being good teachers: that is they must be good in the sense of being effective in terms of the competences required, but also good in the sense of being morally good and possessing the virtues of prudence, temperance, justice and fortitude. Two of the more routine competences that new teachers must attain illustrate this. Section 2.5 of DfE (1992) specifies among other things that teachers must be able to 'assess and record systematically the progress of individual pupils ... and use such assessment in their teaching.'

At first sight, nothing could be more straightforward and mechanical: some (futile) approaches to assessment in the National Curriculum have treated assessment as if it were a clerical task, ticking boxes on forms and piling up boxes of evidence. To be carried out objectively, assessment in terms of the DfE's apparently simple competences requires virtues: prudence, in being concerned for and careful of the consequences of decisions, and appropriately cautious and circumspect; justice, in being impartial and treating all with equity, honesty and fairness; temperance, in maintaining calmness and moderation, and resisting any temptation to hasty decisions or excessive conclusions; fortitude, in having the strength of will to act upon the results of assessment in ways that might require us to modify our own practice, and the resolution, moral courage and firmness of mind to carry the effort through. To learn from experience requires these virtues, and those without virtue lack the capacity to learn. This explains why it is possible for some people to have experiences from which they do not learn: perhaps those who visited the Soviet system or experienced apartheid and found them democratic and civilized lacked one or more of these basic virtues.

It is sometimes asserted that learning requires experience plus reflection on that experience: only what the mind processes remains as learning. On this definition such a luminary as Adolf Hitler was a good learner: he lived through terrible times, he reflected on them and wrote a book, but what he learned, or failed to learn, created the horrors which brought about his own demise. Hegel wrote: 'What experience and history teach us is this – that people and governments never have learnt anything from history, or acted on principles deduced from it.' Perhaps we do not learn, if we do not, because we are not virtuous enough.

The concept of teaching implies that it must be a virtuous activity. Many teachers are unhappy about calling someone a good teacher merely because they are effective in causing something to be learned. The means used and the aims in view seem to be essential components of teaching: it has to be an intrinsically worthwhile or ethically good activity.

RAISING MORALE

The first step in raising teachers' morale is to accept that teachers do not get the support they deserve from the media and Parliament, and to try to understand why. Perhaps it is a consequence of overfamiliarity: we all have more extensive experience of classrooms than we do of surgeries and courts. Perhaps it is a consequence of other people's problems, not those of teachers: negative, mean-spirited attitudes make their first sustained appearance in adolescence, as young people become self-obsessed, criticize their parents and experiment with the role of outsider. If we hypothesize that a substantial proportion of those single-minded people who achieve power and influence in our society are those whose social development has not progressed since their adolescence, many mysteries, as well as hostility to teachers, begin to unravel: the greed, the fraud, the deception, the arrogance, the intimidatory and bullying styles of management. These people need to have regular reports of ineffective teachers (and others who dedicate themselves to helping the victims of our 'me-first' society) to distract them from their own venality and prop up their view of themselves as knowledgeable, worldly and good. Often, these are the people who are prominent in Parliament and the media, and who would like to impose their own virtual-reality on the rest of us.

The atmosphere of crisis in education that has been generated bears little relation to the facts as perceived by parents. Evidence from MORI polls indicates that positive views of schools and their teachers, however scarce among our leaders and would-be opinion-formers, are not hard to find among the general public. Writing in *The Times Educational Supplement* in June 1994, Ben Page (a director of the MORI social research unit) noted that 95 per cent of parents think well of English teaching, for example; and even in deprived and difficult districts, 80 per cent think that their children's education is good. A significant finding, in relation to the argument that misinformation lies behind the media's poor view of schools, is that parents who see most of actual schools think most highly of them. Some of the few parents with negative views of schools were found to base their opinion on incorrect, hearsay information.

Achieving high teacher morale is important. How we feel about ourselves and our work affects our motivation and perception: these will be high and positive where morale is high; and they will be low and pessimistic where morale is low. Teachers who have high morale will tend to be more effective in their teaching, have better relationships with their pupils, and be more co-operative and trusting with others in the education system. Teachers with low morale will be more likely to show a high degree of failure and frustration, be abrasive and confrontational, and suspicious of colleagues, parents and policy-makers. One might review the occasional extreme behaviour of some teacher-union representatives in this light: 'Give a dog an ill name and hang him'; and it may be added, 'if you give a man or race of men an ill name, they are very likely to do something that deserves hanging.' (So wrote Sir Walter Scott, in *Guy Mannering*, in 1815 – more succinctly than our contemporary theorists of labelling and stereotyping.)

These characteristics do not imply any diminution in commitment: a high degree of commitment to one's work, in an atmosphere of disparagement, is a formula productive of low morale. High pay and rewarding conditions of work can buy more than just freedom from union action: teachers who feel rewarded will tend to work harder, achieve more, be less defensive and more self-critical, and less likely to blame others for shortcomings in schools. As W. Edwards Deming, whose writings on management have rightly brought him near-divine status in some parts of the world, puts it: 'The prime requirement for the achievement of any aim, including quality, is joy in work' (Neave, 1990). He quotes Ecclesiastes in support: 'There is no happiness but to be happy in work, for that is the lot given to all people' (3:22).

A report for the National Association of Headteachers (Earley and Baker, 1989) found low morale associated with hasty and ill considered reforms, paperwork, bureaucracy, poor attitudes in the media and the lack of a clear career structure. The authors concluded that there was 'a need for greater recognition, by all parties, of the demands and constraints of the job.' This recognition should include salary levels, administrative support and opportunities for in-service training and staff development. Evidence in the report indicates that, although high morale is sustained by good school relationships, low morale, among senior staff at least, is associated with external, national influences: this further supports the view that ill-considered carping does serious harm. Headteachers in the survey gave a fairly consistent picture of the action needed: better support and resourcing from local and national government, positive images of the profession in the media, and better salaries and conditions of service.

THE INFLUENCE OF DIFFICULT PUPILS

So far we have considered the contribution of external factors. For many teachers (upwards of 38 per cent according to my small survey) the unruly behaviour of some pupils weakens their resolve and handicaps their ability to cope with low public esteem. Although advice on coping with difficult behaviour is plentiful, few authors pay any attention to the needs of the teacher. We will focus on methods of coping with the stresses created by misbehaviour and then return to the external factors to see how these ideas can help in their management; in many ways the lack of respect for teachers that characterizes a minority of adults has its counterpart in the truculence and hostility of a minority of pupils.

Some pupils perceive the classroom as an extension of the uncaring and unforgiving world that they have grown up in: harsh, unjust and unpredictable, characterized by a level of stress, poverty, indifference or cruelty that most of us never encounter. Schools offer a relatively safe environment for such pupils to work through their anger and insecurity. It colonizes their minds and spoils their appreciation of even the most exciting and well-conducted lessons. Teachers have to cope and most do, trying, as Pring did to educate pupils who, in spite of their poor behaviour, have 'minds that questioned, puzzled, doubted, drew conclusions ...' (Pring, 1975). Cronk (1987) took this argument a stage further in attempting to elicit the co-operation of an ill-disciplined class. She hypothesized that ignorance and misunderstanding prevented pupils co-operating with teachers. Getting pupils to accept her own position in the school, bounded as it was by colleagues' expectations and other constraints, helped elicit good behaviour: pupils and teacher came to share their intentions, reasons, feelings and constraints. Perhaps this is why parents are understanding of schools and generally favourably disposed to them.

Stott (1982) believed pupils' hostility to adults was usually an extension of hostility to parents, and that children need a secure attachment to a loyal, dependable, caring parent figure. Those who are thwarted in this need react badly to teachers. It would be an interesting enquiry to research the early lives of public figures who are hostile to teachers. There are tantalizing clues in the memoirs of some of them which suggest that worldly success is correlated with early domestic coolness and strife.

These are no more than speculations. The work of Dreikurs (1957) supplies a tool with much greater explanatory power. This involves trying to identify and analyse pupils' motives and using this information to guide teachers' responses and strategies. The correct identification of motive is a condition precedent to effective action, but the process of identification soothes the teacher even if no effective action is possible. Dreikurs proposes four goals of disturbing behaviour which he relates to the child's experience in the family. Balson (1982), developing the theme, says: 'All maladjustment has its origin in a basic loss of confidence.' Attention-seeking results where young children have done badly in the competition with siblings for parental attention: 'Children prefer being beaten to being ignored' (Balson, 1982, p. 13). Efforts to control the child result in struggles for power in which there can be no final victory, for to win is to teach that power struggles are valuable and worthwhile. This struggle can develop, where parents are bent on victory at any price, into mutual revenge.

Dreikurs says that the same behaviour can serve different motives and each child may have different purposes from time to time. For example, being lazy can be an attention-seeking strategy; it can be a struggle for power with a teacher; it can be revenge upon an ambitious parent. The same child might seek revenge upon overjudgemental parents by being disruptive at school and disappointing them; he or she might try to get sympathetic attention at home by being passive, quiet and withdrawn. The inevitable clash of view between home and school on his or her behaviour would satisfy the child's wish for power. Two clues are available to us in identifying the pupil's motive and knowing how to respond. First, observing one's own feelings: if irritated, attention-seeking; if challenged, power; if outraged, revenge. The teacher's 'automatic reaction is generally in line with what the child wants her to do' (Dreikurs, 1957). Second, observing the child's reaction to correction: if the behaviour stops momentarily, attention; if it continues, power; if it gets much worse, revenge.

Much difficult behaviour in classrooms is described as attention-seeking. If the child is using an unacceptable repertoire only to gain attention, then it is likely that the teacher will feel no more than mildly irritated. Balson suggests that the child is saying 'I'm special, attend to me.' Such behaviour is likely to stop when attention is given and resume as soon as the teacher turns to others in the class. The strategy most likely to succeed here is to be watchful and exploit opportunities to give attention to the attention-seeker when he or she is engaged on the proper tasks. As far as is possible the unwanted behaviour should be ignored or only partially attended to. For example, the child may be instructed to resume the proper seat and wait, but the teacher avoids eye-contact, giving only the minimal attention necessary to the delivery of the instruction. Dreikurs suggests giving attention but in unexpected ways: for example, instead of telling off someone who repeatedly falls off their chair, invite the class to stop work and watch. He suggests disclosing the pupil's motives to him or her in a non-accusatory style ('Could it be that you want to keep me busy ...?') and agreeing a fixed number of times for special attention ('Ten times enough? Okay, that's one'). Explicit rules are not possible of course, and Dreikurs notes 'each teacher must experiment ... and establish her own technique' (Dreikurs, 1957).

What appears to be, and is typed as, attention-seeing may in fact stem from different motives and produce stronger and more distressing responses in the teacher. If the teacher feels the pupil's behaviour is a threat to his or her authority, and feels angrily impelled to force the child into line, then the pupil's motive is power. Both pupil and teacher are likely to be feeling that they must show the other that they cannot be dominated. Balson advises that the impulse to fight is best resisted, thus depriving the pupil of an opponent, and reducing the likelihood of such an unsuccessful pupil strategy being repeated. Dreikurs suggests encouraging a power-seeker to exercise it in legitimate ways: for example, help and protection for others, but discreetly supervised. Openly admitting that the teacher ultimately has no real power can also disarm the pupil.

To resist habitual impulses is not easy and extinguishing unwanted power-seeking behaviour in this way may take some considerable time. Any discomfort or uncertainty shown by the teacher rewards the pupil's efforts and gives the pleasure of victory without a struggle. Other pupils are unlikely to remain unaffected by these phenomena. To be convincing the teacher must genuinely feel unchallenged, so that without the need of speech, he or she communicates imperturbability. This is easier to achieve if we recognize the discouraged and 'frightened child behind all the manifestations of grandeur' (Dreikurs, 1957). Dreikurs points out that children rarely understand 'the predicament in which the teacher finds herself as a result of her exposure to so many pressures' and advises giving the pupil a sense of significance by showing the pupil that she has the power to help.

A further escalation in motivational intensity is evidenced when the teacher feels more deeply hurt and unjustly treated. In such cases the child may be seeking revenge for some real or imagined hurt in the present or a past situation. The child is seeking to even the score and the offended teacher may feel urged to do likewise. This impulse must be resisted if the child is even to consider abandoning this strategy. Dreikurs observes that the support of other pupils, all that the teacher wins in struggles with revenge-seekers, can serve to further isolate the individual. It takes a great deal of stamina to convince the revengeful child that he or she can be liked.

When confronted by behaviour of this sort, which may or may not turn out to be attention-seeking, it is helpful to have a four-point strategy in mind. First, the feelings and emotional reaction produced in the teacher by the pupil's behaviour are probably intentionally so produced. Second, the automatic impulse to respond in a habitual fashion, perhaps in kind, is a signal to pause and reflect on the pupil's motives and intentions. Third, the teacher's own feelings and impulses are a clue to the pupil's state of mind and may be a mirror image of them. Fourth, in order to deprive the pupil of success in his or her attempt at manipulating the teacher's reaction, the teacher must take control: this involves rejecting the normal impulse and dodging the pupil's snare, however painful the necessary agility. Such a strategy takes seconds to describe but will normally operate in a fraction of that time. It is not suggested that teachers who are responsible for pupils should respond to crises with passivity and a caricature of thought. Crisis are to be accepted as inevitable increments of progress: the term does indicate a turning-point, and knowledgeably and carefully handled a crisis becomes a turning-point from which progress follows (Hanko, 1985).

Focusing on the mental and emotional state of pupils does not lead to easily listed techniques or explicit guides to action. Caspari (1976) cautions against expecting to acquire perfect understanding and points out that 'the wish to understand our children and ourselves in relationship to them has a profound effect on this relationship and on our ability to deal with troublesome children.' This approach, however, does benefit both pupil and teacher. It necessitates considering the pupil seriously as another thinking person and reflecting upon the pupil's point of view. To adopt this approach is to communicate to the pupil, not necessarily in words, that he or she is seen as significant, important and deserving time and effort to understand. Pupils learn that their surface behaviour, over which some fear they do not have complete control, will not be accepted as a complete reflection of their personal qualities and feelings.

A policy of understanding pupils has benefits for teachers but it also extends their professional responsibilities. Learning to analyse pupils' mental and emotional dispositions is necessarily learning to adopt a dispassionate and objective perspective. On learning of a pupil's fears we come to see behaviour in a different light (Hanko, 1985). Understanding is partial insulation from personal involvement of a painful and overwhelming kind. Teachers can understand why they are the focus of pupils' confused and misdirected feelings and not perceive such feelings as personal attacks. They can side-step antagonism, focusing their concern instead on pupils' deeper motives. They may also understand why some sorts of behaviour and attitude distress them more than others, for no one is wholly exempt from inner conflicts and uncertainty. It becomes easier to see difficult behaviour as part of ordinary life and, for many pupils, a necessary manifestation of their present concerns. Coping with conflict is seen, not as grit in a machine that would otherwise work smoothly, but as one part of teachers' professional responsibilities: an aspect of the job, not an impediment to it.

We will now apply Dreikurs's two-stage scheme to the assaults on teachers' morale that do not come from pupils. How do teachers feel when they read attacks on their work and achievements in the media? Are we able to discern what effect teachers' reproofs have? The most common response seems to be anger and a feeling of challenge.

'I would say my initial reaction, it was I was furious, incandescent. I thought How dare he, What does that jerk know about me?'

'Despair mostly, and anger, but what can you do, they've got the power and if you, if you try to put your side, no one's listening.'

'I don't, (politicians) don't bother me really, they used to but what really, the thing that really upset me, it was a letter in the *Post*. It was a stupid letter from some idiot going on about our easy day and long holidays and how we should be made to clean up schools and pick litter from the grounds instead of holidays – set an example to the kids we haven't brought up properly to know right from wrong. I ask you, it was probably from someone who spends his evenings watching filthy crap on the TV. But I admit I felt insulted and deeply, in a sort of way, like hurt.'

All but a couple of responses mentioned anger or challenge, indicating that they correctly felt the power-motive that lies behind most attacks on the teaching profession. Attaching themselves to this publicly sanctioned enterprise are a small number of unpleasant people who are seeking revenge for their own scholastic failures. Such a one, though demonstrably foolish, was able to evoke feelings of being wounded in one teacher. Pupils of similar ineptitude are also capable of disturbing the most conscientious of professionals. One teacher quoted above recognized the futility of responding to attacks, and in so doing demonstrated the second stage of Dreikurs's scheme in operation: ordinary attempts at correction fail and those seeking power persist in their efforts.

This knowledge, derived by using Dreikurs's strategy, should help teachers cope better with unjust criticism, in the same way that it helps them cope with difficult and challenging pupils. It also suggests, at least tentatively, how teachers should respond.

First, recognize that many punishing attacks on teaching and hostile feelings towards teachers come from those who live in a harsh and unforgiving world in which they have suffered disappointments – as all who remain in the self-centred anger of adolescence must do. Recognize that their hostile feelings are their problem, not yours, and try to explain the constraints under which teachers work.

Second, abandon open struggles with power-motivated, political attacks. Stick to dispassionate statements of the truth: on the whole there is nothing wrong with teaching or teachers; but there is something worrying, in a democracy, about those who want to tighten their grip on a profession that could be used (and has been) to mould young minds in unhealthy ways. It is not an educational problem but a political one.

Third, build up the evidence which supports professional standards and expand links with those who are likely to give their support objectively and fairly. For example, there is anecdotal evidence that the use of lay-inspectors on inspection teams (intended to keep untrustworthy professionals in check) has improved the understanding that such outsiders have for teachers and schools. Far from acting as a control, the introduction of lay-inspectors has increased their respect for teachers and the conditions in which they have to work.

Fourth, build links with high-status outsiders who can be expected to be fair and objective. Teachers now have stronger links with higher education than ever through their statutory involvement in teacher training and their role as quasi-members of university staffs. This could be developed to teachers' further advantage by a new range of high-status higher degrees which accredit expertise in classrooms. Such degrees would have two elements: the demonstration of excellence in practical teaching; and the preparation of a practical, curriculum or school-related project. Superior teaching could be determined by OFSTED-trained, university assessors who would watch lessons, inspect pupils' work and results and talk to employers and pupils. The written project could take many forms but would be a substantial document usable by other teachers and not a detached academic exercise: it might be a collection of lectures, a textbook, an individual programme for a disabled pupil, or an instruction manual for organizing a first-class nursery. Both elements would give a rounded picture of teaching excellence and ought therefore to merit the highest academic awards that universities can confer. A growing number of doctors of teaching would be beacons of excellence, inspiring their colleagues and providing tangible evidence of the academic regard for the profession. As the pilot advised, if you want to boost morale, light a fire.

REFERENCES

Angyalfi, S. (1994) *The historical development of Jewish special education*. Thesis, Leeds Metropolitan University.

Balson, M. (1982) *Understanding Classroom Behaviour*. Hawthorn, Victoria: Australian Council for Education Research.

Caspari, I. (1976) *Troublesome Children in Class*. London: Routledge and Kegan Paul.

Cronk, K. A. (1987) *Teacher-Pupil Conflict in Secondary Schools*. Lewes: Falmer.

DfE (Department for Education) (1992) *Initial Teaching Training (Secondary Phase)*. Circular 9/92. London: Department for Education.

Dreikurs, R. (1957) *Psychology in the Classroom*. London: Staples Press.

Earley, P. and Baker, L. (1989) *The Recruitment, Retention, Motivation and Morale of Senior Staff in Schools*. London: NFER (National Foundation for Educational Research).

Elton Report (1989) *Discipline in Schools*. Report of the Committee of Enquiry chaired by Lord Elton. London: HMSO.

Gillborn, D., Nixon, J. and Ruddock, J. (1993) *Dimensions of Discipline, Rethinking Practice in Secondary Schools*. London: Department for Education.

Hanko, G. (1985) *Special Needs in Ordinary Classrooms*. Oxford: Basil Blackwell.

King, R. (1978) *All things Bright and Beautiful?* London: Wiley.

McManus, M. and Metcalfe, C. *Values and Teaching*. Leeds Metropolitan University Monograph in preparation.

National Curriculum Council (NCC) (1989) *Curriculum for All: Special Needs in the National Curriculum*. London: HMSO.

Neave, H. R. (1990) *The Deming Dimension*. Knoxville Tennessee: SPCC Press.

OFSTED, (1993), *Standards and Quality in Education 1992–93*. London: OFSTED.

OFSTED (1995) *The Annual Report of Her Majesty's Chief Inspector of Schools*. London: HMSO.

Pring, R. (1976) *Knowledge and Schooling*. London: Open Books.

Stott, D. H. (1982) *Helping the Maladjusted Child*. Milton Keynes: Open University Press.

Name Index

Subject Index

Also available from Cassell:

R. Best, P. Lang and A. Lichtenberg (eds): *Caring for Children*
R. Best, P. Lang, C. Lodge and C. Watkins (eds): *Pastoral Care and PSE*
D. Child: *Psychology and the Teacher* (5th edition)
C. Clark: *Thoughtful Teaching*
A. Hargreaves and M. Fullan (eds): *Understanding Teacher Development*
E. Hoyle and P. John: *Professional Knowledge and Professional Practice*
J. Jones and J. Mathias: *Training for Appraisal and Professional Development*
I. Lawrence (ed.): *Education Tomorrow*
A. Pollard and S. Tann: *Reflective Teaching in the Primary School* (2nd edition)
J. Sayer: *Secondary Schools for All* (2nd edition)
R. Smith: *Successful School Management*
R. Smith: *The Future Governance of Education*
V. Varma (ed.): *Coping with Unhappy Children*

12.99

THE NEEDS OF TEACHERS